HOSTA

HOSTAGE

GLEN DIXON

as told to Anthony Mockler

Columbus Books
London

First published in Great Britain in 1986 by
Columbus Books
Devonshire House, 29 Elmfield Road, Bromley, Kent BR1 1LT

British Library Cataloguing in Publication Data
Dixon, Glen
Hostage
1. Hostages—Angola—History—20th century
2. Angola—History—1975–
I. Title II. Mockler, Anthony
967'.304'0924 DT611.8

ISBN 0–86287–271–5

Phototypeset by Falcon Graphic Art Ltd
Wallington, Surrey
Printed and bound by
Mackays of Chatham Ltd, Kent

DEDICATION

To the families that waited. . .
To the lads that walked

Contents

List of illustrations (between pages 64 and 65)

ANGOLA
a note on the background

The country through which Glen Dixon and his companions made their forced march has been in the grip of civil war for many years.

The conflict is between the government forces, FAPLA (*Forças Armadas Populares de Libertação*), and UNITA (*União Naçional para la Independencia Total de Angola*), the rebel forces. Angola was for almost four hundred years part of Portugal's African empire, and Portuguese is still the country's official language.

The present government is Marxist. It took over the capital of the country, Luanda, when independence was proclaimed on 11 November 1975. But as the Portuguese pulled out, the economy of the country collapsed. Almost 300,000 Portuguese settlers left the country; they, as small farmers, engineers and mechanics, even as taxi-drivers and hotel staff, had run everything.

Quickly Russian 'advisers' moved in to fill the gap – only a few hundred, but they were followed, to the horror of the West, by a Cuban expeditionary force almost 30,000 strong sent by Fidel Castro. These Cuban troops manned the tanks and planes supplied by the Russians, and, fighting side by side with FAPLA, managed to turn the tide in the fierce civil war that was, at the time of Independence, washing around the very outskirts of the capital.

However, Jonas Savimbi, the leader of the pro-Western guerrillas, UNITA, held on in the south of Angola and gradually built up his forces, with help from white South Africa, to something approaching a regular army. This organization controlled one-third or more of the country.

Angola is vast, underpopulated and divided almost in two by the strategic Benguela railway that runs across it from the Atlantic coast on the west to the eastern border with Angola's mighty – and generally hostile – neighbour Zaire (formerly the Congo, but re-christened by its bloodstained ruler President Sese Seko Mobutu). Coffee was once Angola's chief export, but its plantations were abandoned by the Portuguese at the time of Independence, and the labour force has since dispersed or grown old; no knowledge or expertise remained whereby the cultivation of coffee could be revived. The Marxist government depends for its income on two basic sources: the oil of Cabinda Province, an enclave in the far north, and the diamonds of Lunda Norte Province, also in the north and bordering Zaire.

Jonas Savimbi's UNITA forces have for years been trying to put out of action the diamond mines of Lunda Norte Province where Glen Dixon, just one of many expatriates employed in the government-run mining industry, was working at the time of his capture.

A.M.

Chapter 1

The Attack

Outside it was just cracking dawn, with the sky a sort of greyish pink. Inside my house in Cafunfo I was sleeping, dead to the world, in utter darkness. It must have been about a quarter to five. My bed was up against the verandah wall. The first thing I heard was spat-spat-spat on the wall, then suddenly there were bullets whanging through the zinc sheet roof above. 'That's it,' I said to myself. 'We're in trouble.'

There was absolutely no doubt in my mind what was happening. I didn't even have time to think 'Jesus, this is UNITA!' or anything like that. I was expecting it somehow, subconsciously. As soon as I woke up I thought, 'Bugger! They're here.' I'll never forget that day: it was the last Saturday in 1984, one of the longest days in my life.

For the first few minutes it was all action. All my windows were boarded up to prevent thieving: I had had shutters put on and they were all screwed into place from the outside. So I slept in total blackness and could not see out. As I leapt out of bed bullets were whanging all over the place and there were crumps as mortars landed – some close, some not so far away. I went into the lounge, without knowing why, then I ran back into the bedroom and got dressed. Luckily I'm an orderly person and I had everything to hand, though knowing what I know now I think I would have slowed down and dressed properly for the occasion. At any rate, that's my advice to anyone else caught in a similar position: take very good care what you wear because you may be wearing that, and nothing else, for a long time to come. I had a lot of brand-new gear lying in the cupboard that my wife Lynn had brought out from England for me, but I put on my old things: a pair of blue-jean shorts over the underpants I'd been sleeping in (I never wear long trousers in Africa), a khaki army shirt with lapels and a company badge above the breast pocket, a thin pair of socks, which were to prove a disaster, and town boots with high heels, 1-inch heels. (You'll hear more about them later, because what you put on your feet in situations like that in which I found myself is probably the single most important decision you have to take.)

I stuffed my sunglasses down the inside of my shirt – that was lucky, as it turned out – put my reading glasses in the breast pocket and grabbed a new packet of cigarettes, a gas lighter and a cigarette filter. Best of all, I remembered a hat. Then I ran out of the bedroom, through the lounge, and opened the front door.

As I opened the front door, a 2-inch mortar landed in my back yard and blew the back door off its hinges. It was lucky I was already going out; but what with the momentum and the air pressure I did a quick flip through the verandah gate, and then I was running up the road.

As I ran I could see all these pink things shooting across the roofs of the houses. 'This is bloody daft!' I remember thinking. Then there was a gap between the houses, and all these things were whizzing in front of my eyes. Again I thought, 'This is crazy.' I knew what they were, of course. I had been in the army. 'What the hell are they using tracer for?' I wondered; but I did not really think of it in terms of the danger I was in. What *did* frighten me as I ran up that road was a mortar landing in a back garden. I turned round and I saw the pawpaw tree (a big one), the zinc sheet roof and everything flying up in the air. 'Bugger me,' I thought, 'that is the end of John' (John MacMichael – the engineer who lived in the house). But it wasn't. John slept right through it. He reckoned afterwards that he slept for half an hour after the attack began – and the mortar landed only about three minutes after it had started. How he managed that I still can't imagine. And when he did finally wake up, he didn't know what was going on – he thought it was maybe FAPLA, the government forces, having a riot. Of course he had only been in Angola two or three weeks, so he wasn't expecting an attack as the rest of us were; nor did he know how jumpy the FAPLA garrison was, the very soldiers who were meant to be defending us.

The reason I was running so hard was not to get away from my house, nor out of blind panic, but to reach my Filipino lads. They worked under me for my company, Intraco, as mechanics and suchlike, and had been specially imported to Angola by us. I felt responsible for them – all seventeen of them. They lived in two compounds, most of them in the junior compound towards which I was heading.

Francis was what they called their 'grandfather', their

'abuelo', the senior Filipino. A fine lad, 47 years old, with an infectious giggle, he had been in Angola three years. He spoke both English and Portuguese, and he could always keep the Filipinos' morale up.

'O.k., everybody,' I said, bursting into the room where they were sleeping. 'Lie flat on the floor. Stay on the floor.'

They were awake, of course. They knew exactly what was going on. I'd always told them to keep their personal gear handy in case we had to move off *rapido*. But they were really nervous. Few of them had ever been under fire before.

'Wait for me to come back,' I said. 'Don't move. Just lie on the floor.'

Then Francis piped up: 'What about throwing a white sheet over the verandah?'

'Good idea,' I replied.

So he and I stripped a sheet off a bed, went out to the front of the house and pushed the sheet over the edge of the verandah.

'O.k., make sure nobody gets up and nobody moves,' I told Francis. 'Wait till I come back.'

Across the road from the Filipinos' junior compound was our canteen, where we all messed. Cookie was there.

'What shall I do, boss?' he asked.

'Stay here till I get back,' I shouted. Then I went over the wall of the English lads' garden to the senior Filipinos' house.

'Everybody lie on the floor till I come back,' I told them. So that was the Filipinos sorted out.

All this takes time to tell but in fact it can hardly have been ten minutes since I was woken up. Then I crossed the road and went into the house of Jim Taggart, another colleague.

The door was wide open. Jim was up and dressed, but in a state.

Once again, I was asked: 'What shall we do?'

'Put the bloody kettle on, Jim,' I replied. 'Let's have a cup of tea. I'm sodding dying of thirst.'

That may seem a bit strange with all this firing and mortaring going on; after all, we did not have much time to get organized if we were to escape before UNITA captured the town, or a pitched battle broke out with us in the middle of it, or whatever. But I had never needed a cup of tea so badly as I did then; and the same was true of Jim, I think. Then, as he was putting the kettle on, something struck me.

'Have you radioed, Jim?' I asked.

'Radioed who?'

'Radioed Dundo,' I answered impatiently.

'No,' he replied. 'I never gave it a thought.'

In his bedroom there was this high-frequency two-way radio, so we rushed down the corridor to his bedroom and switched the radio on.

'Dundo, Dundo, come in Dundo,' he began.

'Jim,' I interrupted, 'it's just after 5 a.m. Nobody's going to be there. Just go "Mayday, Mayday" across the waveband till somebody answers you.'

So he began maydaying across the wavebands. All of a sudden the power started to go off. It picked up again, then it faded, and that was it: all the power went off. The radio was powered by our generators, so that meant the attacking force must have blown the generators – and that, incidentally, meant that the electric kettle had gone off, too, so there was no tea either.

Jim and I looked at each other. We went out into the back yard. All the fire was coming in from the east, nothing from the south or north or west. We'd been making a swimming-pool base in the back yard there, and it was that that probably saved our lives then. As we were watching, an RPG – a rocket-propelled grenade – came plopping down on this site. It just made a small hole, about 6 inches in diameter, in the sand. Had it been a hard base it would have exploded and shattered everything around, us included.

'Those things are dangerous,' I said, idiotically. 'They can kill you if they catch you in the open.' People get a bit idiotic at moments like that. They don't know what they are saying. Then I pulled myself together. 'Come on, Jim, this is no place for us. Back into the house.' We moved fast, believe me.

Once we were safely back inside, Jim turned to me and said, 'Let's get away.'

'Right. Give me ten minutes, Jim. Just let me collect all the Filipinos together, and I'll be with you.'

As it happened, that was easier said than done. The senior Filipinos had locked themselves in, so I couldn't get into their compound, and by the time I was back in the junior Filipinos' compound, having just been missed by a mortar, I was shattered. I had been running on adrenalin for the past fifteen minutes but I had weight on – I must have weighed about 14 or

15 stone at the time – and I thought I was going to have a heart attack from over-exertion. I lay there in the corridor panting till I had got my breath back.

'We're going across the road, lads, into Jim Taggart's house,' I said. 'No problem across the compound, but spread out and go across the road one by one, not in a gang. Francis, you start them going.'

I brought up the rear. They were all teetering by the gate, bunched up, and I had to push them across one by one. As I went through a mortar hit the wall behind us. A bit of shrapnel took a slice out of my boot, but it was only a scratch. We picked up Cookie en route and I tried to get the senior Filipinos again, but couldn't. By the time I was in Jim Taggart's house and shouting, 'Jim!' he had gone.

So I herded the Filipinos into the corridor that ran down the centre of his house, the safest place, and made them all lie down again while I dashed around outside, looking for him, trying to find out what was going on, and nearly getting shot up again in the process too.

Jim Taggart was in his fifties, 55 or 56, a very thin, wiry guy and he'd been in Africa quite a few years, got on well with Africans and knew his way around; but he didn't have any bushcraft: that was his big disadvantage. He had in fact managed to escape, and later on I heard how he did it. He had waited the ten minutes we'd stipulated and then, when I didn't get back in time, he went over the wall, over the road, down the runway past the carpenter's shop, crossed the runway under fire, then lay up in the long grass about 300 yards past the airstrip. He lay there in the pouring rain for three days and three nights, with nothing to eat or drink and pestered by mosquitoes. Then on the fourth day, when all firing seemed to have stopped, he headed west to the Cuango river ten miles away. There he was picked up on the Friday, six days after the attack. He had lost a stone and a half. Still, nerve-wracking though that was, he had an easier time than Peter Hewitt.

Peter was about a year or so younger than Jim, about 54, but he was pretty fit, a big lad. He wasn't carrying a lot of fat on him. I think he had been in Angola about six years. He was in the English lads' house and he hid in the roof – this was a proper house with beams and panels – without food or water for three days. The biggest worry for him, apart from the bombing, was that UNITA occupied the house for those three days. On three occasions they even searched the loft, but they never found him. As I understand it, when he got out he met up with some Angolans and walked with them along the road. But he was in a very bad condition. He spent about ten days in hospital, and they had to bring special drugs out from the UK for him. I think it was his nerves more than anything. He didn't go home on leave even when he was safely back in civilization, in Dundo. He stayed on in Angola, looking – I was told – as if he had aged ten years.

Two others who escaped (Jim Taggart met up with them briefly as they ran for it) were two Portuguese who lived on the other side of town. They were mining foremen. One of them was a very down-to-earth Portuguese called David, a construction foreman who used to go drinking with the Angolans. The other was the welding foreman. Another Portuguese who escaped, with his wife and kids, was a local farmer. I actually saw him myself careering out of town in his Land Rover as I ran across the road. (Later we saw this Land Rover in UNITA's possession and wondered what had happened to the family.) But of course this story isn't about the ones who escaped. If we had escaped too there would have been no story to tell.

We might have escaped, though, if we'd moved earlier. I had the lads ready to move out, planning to head west, when firing started coming in from the north and south. Well, Gorden Bennett, I said to myself, UNITA are moving round. They're planning to cut us off, and if we start moving now we'll likely enough get caught in crossfire between the two sides.

'Right, lads, back in the house,' I said.

Heavy machine-gun fire was hitting the walls now. They were only red-brick, and hollow, but fortunately they were lined with cement both sides so they offered good protection.

'We've missed our chances of escaping by about five minutes,' I told them. 'The only thing to do now is lie still and wait till FAPLA win or UNITA win, whichever.'

We lay there while the battle raged on. Bullets were coming through the windows and hitting the walls, blasting through the doors above us. Then the noise died off. Sometimes there was just a single shot: bang! bang! Then it would start up again. Philip – he was the youngest of the Filipinos, only 22, the only unmarried one – had gone a ghastly grey. He stuck to me like a leech. Every time I shifted position, he shifted too. I tried to calm him down and give him a bit of confidence.

'We're all right here, lads,' I said. 'They've been throwing the lot at us, but they can't get us in this passage.'

Ephraim put his finger on it, though. A very sensible type of lad he was, very calm. He knew the real problem.

'How do you reckon we are going to surrender?' he asked.

'You're right,' I answered. 'If UNITA win, the biggest problem is going to be surrender. At the moment we are o.k. Just leave it and let's work it out as we go.' It seemed the best thing to say.

At the time, of course, we had no idea at all who was winning. As we lay in that corridor I suddenly thought about my pantry, which I'd converted into a strongroom. There were a quarter of a million cigarettes there – Benson & Hedges and Marlboro. But it wasn't that which was worrying me, it was the rest of the contents. There were about 60 bottles of whisky, 40 bottles of gin and about 20 bottles of other alcohol. Christ, I thought, if this bunch of hooligans smashes my place and gets into that liquor store, we have had it. There is nothing worse than a drunken African with a gun.

But the only thing we could do at the time was to try and make jokes. I remember at one point I crawled into the bathroom, and there were two lads actually in the bath. One was lying down with his back in the bottom of the bath and Francis was lying on top of him. I came in on my hands and knees and saw his bum sticking out of the bath.

'Bloody hell, Francis,' I said, 'I didn't know you had gone bent!' I was trying to make a joke out of it but it wasn't appreciated.

'Francis,' I said, more seriously, 'if the bullets come through that wall they are going to take your backside off – and your feet.'

So out he popped and down on to the floor again.

One consolation was that we all had plenty of cigarettes. We just lay there smoking like troopers – and, in my case, longing for a cup of tea. It was still pretty cool. The time must have been not far off 7.30 a.m. and the firing had more or less stopped. This is it, I thought: whoever has won will be around shortly.

Ephraim stood up.

'Ephraim,' I said, 'lie down on the floor. It's not over yet.'

Sure enough, just as he lay back on the floor an RPG hit the corner of the lounge. All the brickwork caved in, brick ends bouncing off Filipinos, dust everywhere. We couldn't see anything. We let it settle and just lay there frozen, waiting.

Then there was silence. The next thing I heard was a voice shouting, 'Glen!'

'Yes,' I shouted back.

'Where are you?'

'Jim Taggart's house.'

It was John MacMichael.

John had had a really frightening experience. As I said, he hadn't woken up till half an hour after the attack started, and even then he hadn't realized properly what was going on. John has a very high metabolism and needs a lot of food, so he had gone into the kitchen, grabbed what he could find and really stuffed himself. His nerves were working on him and he was starving. Not that John was a nervous type. He was an Ulsterman, a very quiet lad, about 5 foot 10 and very thin. He'd been out of Ireland seven years, having emigrated when he was 21, as soon as he left university. He had an engineering degree and he had just wanted to get out of Ireland. His father was dead, his sister was married and living in Scotland and he only had his mother, who was very independent. So he took a chance and emigrated to South Africa.

In one of the arguments we had he said to me: 'You bloody Scorpios are all the same.'

'Now what's got you?' I asked.

'You are exactly like my mother. She's a Scorpio, too.'

'What has that got to do with it?'

'She always tries to make decisions for me and tell me what to do,' he said indignantly, 'and you are just the bloody same.'

That was later, of course, when we had got to know each other well. At this time we hardly knew each other at all, other than to speak to.

So, after he had stuffed himself, John crawled back into his lounge on his hands and knees and lay under his bed. He lay there for a long time until the firing died down and it went quiet outside. Then, all of a sudden, his front door was shot off its hinges and he could hear bullets pouring through. John crawled out from under his bed and stuck his head round the bedroom door to see what was going on. He could see the front door, and a rifle, and a bloke coming in.

'*Britannico!*' John cried out.

The bloke swung round as soon as he heard John's voice, and pulled the trigger. The bullets hit the wall above John's head, so he whipped his head back in smartish, crawled back and lay flat under the bed again. Then the gunman edged forward, stuck the gun barrel round the edge of the bedroom door and let a whole magazine rip. He sprayed the whole room with bullets. John was screaming '*Britannico!*' the whole of the time. The bullets went wide but John was hit in the back of the neck by a piece of shrapnel. Sod it, he thought at that point, I'm dead anyway: I'm walking out whether they shoot me or not. So he just stood up calmly and walked through the bedroom door. The gunman brought his rifle up. John could see his finger on the trigger. But the intruder must have been amazed to see a white man. John just said '*Britannico*' again quietly, and that did it. The bloke put his barrel down.

It took John quite a while to get over this episode, because he really believed he had had it that time. John was born in Omagh, and he had been through a lot with the IRA. He had had his back broken with a crowbar, after which three of his vertebrae had to be moulded together. And when he was in hospital he had had a hand grenade thrown under his bed, which blew it up to the ceiling. He has been through a lot, John, but he told me that all the IRA business had never bothered him that much. Yet that morning, with the UNITA bloke – that was the first time he had ever been really scared.

It was lucky for us, really, that John had been captured before we were discovered. After he'd shouted to me and I'd shouted back, there was silence. Then suddenly the double doors leading on to Jim Taggart's verandah were smashed open and eight of these UNITA lads rushed in waving AKs. I just had my head sticking out from the corridor, peering round, and I put my hand out and waved. They were a right bunch of hooligans, a really scruffy lot. Some had only one shoe on, some only one trouser-leg; their shirts were ripped, covered with bandoliers; some had hats, some didn't.

There was a lot of jabbering in Portuguese.

'*Não comprehendo*,' I said; and I stood up slowly with my hands in the air while they went on jabbering.

Then I made a mistake.

Francis speaks pretty good Portuguese, so I said: 'Francis, come out.'

I suddenly realized that Francis looks more Korean than any of the others, and UNITA hate the North Koreans even worse than they hate the Russians or the Cubans. So I said quickly: 'Come out on your hands and knees, Francis. Just stick your head out.'

Fancy picking Francis, I thought to myself. Sure enough the UNITA guy screamed, '*Koreano!*'

'*Não Koreano. Filipino!*' I said; and then, fortunately Francis began talking to him, still on his hands and knees, in Portuguese, explaining the situation.

More and more UNITA were drifting in, this lot with their AKs slung over their shoulders. There could be no doubt at all about who had won the battle.

Francis looked up. 'He wants everybody to stand up and come out,' he told us.

'No,' I replied, thinking quickly. 'Let them all come out on their hands and knees too.'

It looked ridiculous, but I did not want to take any chances. All the Filipinos had bags, and if they had walked out clutching them there was a risk that some trigger-happy UNITA bloke might think they had guns behind their bags and open fire. (In an attack the previous February, two Filipinos had been killed during the surrender.) So they all crawled out, one by one.

They herded us out into the road then, with John. John was in a state of shock, not with it at all. It was about 8 o'clock by this time, nearly three hours since the attack had started.

'Sit down, lads,' I said, because I thought it better to adopt a submissive attitude rather than a more aggressive position, standing up. Even then I wasn't going to take any chances. There were still bullets whanging around and the UNITA lads were pretty excited. They had probably been taking drugs – marijuana – before the attack, and they were still drugged up. There must have been about thirty or thirty-five of them running around. Some were laughing and cheering and shaking hands with each other, but others were in the house shooting through the ceiling, nicking things and generally smashing the place up.

Then one of them turned nasty. He jammed his gun up against the forehead of one of the Filipinos, Fred. I wasn't having that. I got up and pushed the barrel of the gun off his head. It was red hot, that barrel. It left a burn on my hand. The next thing I knew another of them had shoved a rifle under my jaw and forced me down. I was lying flat on the road with this rifle barrel jammed against my jaw. I thought I was a goner, then. I thought he was going to pull the trigger. He kept me like that for two long, long minutes. I could hear Francis talking Portuguese and them jabbering away among themselves in Portuguese and the local tongue. Then the pressure was released. When I sat back up, the same guy had his gun planted on Fred's forehead again.

'What's going on?' I asked Francis, still half-dazed.

Francis looked scared.

'They think he was captured among the last lot from February.'

That was really dangerous. UNITA never, under any circumstances, allowed foreigners who had been captured and then released to come back and work in Angola again. It was always a condition of their release that they had to swear not to return; and we all knew the penalty for oathbreakers.

'Francis,' I said, 'you stand up with me.'

We both stood up.

'Look,' I said to him, 'you translate directly what I say. Tell them nobody here has been in Angola more than six months, nobody at all except you and me.'

Francis told them that; and at last the bloke took his rifle barrel away. But there was more trouble looming. They were dancing and singing and firing off rounds, really over-excited, and they were certainly drugged up. Their eyes were glassy and their pupils were small. They started ripping open the Filipinos' bags. Ephraim got a bit mad about this, as did the electrician, Romeo.

'Look, *calma, calma*,' I told them. 'Just sit down and shut up and let them do what they like, or it could get rough.'

The UNITA soldiers came over to me. One of them took my reading glasses out of my breast pocket, just screwed them up and stamped on them – ground them under his heel. Fortunately UNITA missed my sunglasses. But they took my cigarettes, and my lighter, too. Then they asked me if there were any more people. I pointed at the senior Filipinos' compound.

'There are two old Filipinos and the doctor in that house,' I said. That was Hobart, who at 60 was the oldest of the lot, Ted, and Roddy the doctor. They were still locked in and, I imagine, still hiding and trembling, not knowing what was going on.

Immediately I'd finished speaking, this cretin whirled round and fired about half a magazine through the windows of the house. He started dancing a jig. Then he ran up the steps and smashed the front door down. I thought he was going to massacre them all.

What probably saved their lives was a UNITA officer who suddenly appeared, in the nick of time, dressed in proper military uniform.

'What is the problem?' he asked. He spoke, to my amazement, in English.

When I explained, he shouted at the dancing man, who stopped his antics and came smartly to attention. They were a well disciplined lot, UNITA, not like the FAPLA garrison troops, who never seemed to pay the slightest attention to officers and just slopped around as they wished. Then this officer went into the senior Filipinos' compound and came out with Hobart, Roddy and pot-bellied Ted. I had taken him for a lieutenant, because he had two pips on his green beret, and two pips in the British Army means a lieutenant. But in fact UNITA uses the American system, and those two stars meant he was a lieutenant colonel, the lieutenant colonel commanding the battalion that had captured us.

As he walked off, I shouted after him: 'What are you going to do with us?'

But all he said was, 'Later, later.'

At least we were all together and unwounded, all the Filipinos and me, and John – though John was like a zombie. But the officer's answer to my shouted question was hardly reassuring. Once the officer's back was turned, we were told to stand up, and the Filipinos became really frightened.

'Here it comes,' one of them said to me.

'Here what comes?'

'This is where they are going to shoot us.'

'If they were going to shoot us,' I said, trying to reassure him, and to reassure myself too, 'they would have done that before now.'

'No, boss, they are going to stick us up against a wall and shoot us.'

'No, no,' I said. 'Just take it easy and don't do anything daft. Just stay calm.'

Philip, the youngest, was right tight up to me, hanging on to my shirt sleeve. I had a short-sleeved shirt on, and I could feel him trembling through it. But at this stage I wasn't really too worried myself. After all, I had nearly been killed by tracer bullets and mortars and an RPG during the attack; and then I'd nearly been shot by an infuriated UNITA bloke. So it had been a crowded morning, one way and another. But I was still alive, and had come out of it with only a scratch on my foot and a burn on my hand. I felt we were all going to come through now that we had survived the most dangerous moment of all, the moment of actual capture, and had been seen by an officer. Also, one detail reassured me: UNITA had broken into the pantry and the canteen as I had feared, but though they were walking around with bottles of whisky and gin and cigarettes galore, they had not opened them. They were pretty strict about drinking, and thank Christ for that. The marijuana wasn't a real problem. They had probably used that to give them momentum on the attack. Though they looked scruffy, their discipline was pretty good – and it was hardly surprising they looked such a bunch of hooligans, seeing that they'd been living in the bush, moving up for the attack, for the past nine months, as we found out later.

They did turn nasty again, though, when one of them got hold of one of the Filipinos, lifted his arm, and found he had a watch on – a solid gold Omega. At that, they all piled into us again, the whole lot of them, kicking us and banging us about and ripping our watches off. But it wasn't really malicious: it was just for the watches. All victorious armies loot – that's historical fact. Reading history, about the Boer War, Napoleon and suchlike, is one of my hobbies. That is not to say that I liked being the victim of looting. One cretin came by with the tablecloth out of my house, a box of cassettes and my big JVC radio. Meanwhile there was still a lot of firing going on, but it was impossible to tell whether it was FAPLA fighting back or just these drug-happy yobbos blasting away, or what.

One thing that struck me was that we had not seen any black civilians at all since the attack began. (Later, I found out that most of them had heard there was going to be an attack and had scarpered during the night, even the upper black management.) But now they brought a group of Angolans to join us, mainly girls and young lads (UNITA recruited most of them later on). There was also one upper-management bloke there, the chief of mining operations, with his girlfriend – who was seven months pregnant. That was probably why he had not scarpered himself. I knew him very well, but he sat apart and totally ignored me. In the end he managed to win his release, I learnt later, by pretending he was an assistant labourer working in the stores. If UNITA had found out he was chief of operations, they would certainly have executed him. The whole point of their attacks was to close the diamond mining industry down, and that meant closing the personnel down too if they could.

They also brought in three Portuguese. Ferreira was the leader of the Portuguese group, quite a strong personality and quite a likeable fellow. He spoke a little bit of English and you could hold a very flimsy conversation with him. As time went on, he would come and ask us English words or the equivalent in Portuguese. He was a trier and you had to admire him. He was the strong man among the Portuguese. I would not have liked to have a shindig with Ferreira, because in terms of physical strength I think I would have come off the worse. The other two were really weak characters. One – Antonio, his real name was – we called Silver, because he had a massive crop of silver hair; he had been in charge of the machine shop. The other was an electrical installation foreman; I can't even remember his name. That may seem odd, seeing that we were to be so many weeks together; but because of the language barrier we didn't really have much to do with the Portuguese. They kept themselves to themselves – except for Bushbunny. But I'll come to him later.

They marched us out of town then towards the east, the direction the attack had come in from. As we came by the workshops, we saw all my earth-moving machines (all Intraco's machines, I should say) lined up, reconditioned, ready to go – but the tyres were all shot out and they'd set fire to all of them. It was enough to break my heart, and the Filipinos' too – after all the work we'd put into those machines. But that was their whole purpose in attacking the town, to put the mining industry there out of action, and that meant destroying the installations, and the vehicles too, as far as they could.

The outskirts of the town had been surrounded by a defensive trench system. What had happened was that UNITA had infiltrated the trench system in the east before dawn, surprised and killed the FAPLA troops who were meant to be defending it, then worked their way around the trenches from the east, mounting machine-guns in the north, squeezing the FAPLA garrison out of the trenches and back through the town until eventually UNITA came round to the airstrip in the west. They claimed to have killed about half of the 300-odd FAPLA garrison troops. As we passed out across the trench system in the east, we saw some dead FAPLA lying in the trenches. Some had had their throats cut; they had no gun wounds. Nights were cold in that part of Angola at that time of year, and they were all half-wrapped in blankets – they had probably been asleep when they were killed; as I've said, they were a dozy lot.

Looking at them gave me an idea. I pointed into the trench at the blanket.

'*Amigo, posibile mantel*?' I said to one of the UNITA men.

'*Si*,' he said, '*nada problem*.'

So I said to the Filipinos: 'Grab all the blankets you can, anything you see.'

We piled into those trenches and got about fifteen blankets out altogether. But half of them were drenched in blood, so we just took eight with us in the end.

We went across the fire-strip then. That was about 500 yards wide, like a ploughed field, cleared to give an open field of fire to the FAPLA lads in the trenches. That was a bit worrying. John was just in front of me.

'Leave a space between you and the UNITA lads,' I said to him, 'because if there are any FAPLA still about, we are right in the open and if they open up on UNITA you will go with them.'

UNITA were nervous too. Once in the grass and trees on the other side, we followed a footpath and came across a small mud hut, and they just opened up on it, spraying right through it and back again. 'This doesn't make sense,' I remember thinking. It was a long, straight path. About 500 yards ahead of us a group came out from the grass. 'FAPLA?' we wondered. But our escort – there were about twenty of them – stopped and held their rifles above their heads, and brought them up and down three times: it was their recognition signal, and the other group did the same. Within minutes we had joined up with a load of UNITA camp-followers – women, cooks, nurses and so on.

By this time, of course, it was fairly clear what was going to happen to us. We were not the first foreign workers in Angola to be taken hostage by UNITA, not by a long chalk. But all the same it was soon to be confirmed. About two or three miles further on, in a steep valley, the officer – the lieutenant colonel – caught up with us again.

'What are you going to do with us?' I asked.

'You walk to Jamba,' he replied.

'How far is Jamba?'

'Three or four weeks' walk. No problem, do not worry about anything.'

'The Filipinos think you are going to execute them.'

'No, all of you will go to Jamba.'

I turned round and said to Francis, Ephraim and Roddy the doctor, who were close behind: 'Pass that message back as you heard it, in your own language.'

That reassured the Filipinos, and they all perked up after that. It did not exactly reassure me – a long march through the bush under that bunch of hooligans, roughly from the north of Angola right down to the south, wasn't what I had come to the country for. I thought of making a break for it there and then, but UNITA seemed to be all around us, coming out of the bush from all directions, and in any case I could hardly leave my Filipinos. On thinking it over I warned them against it too.

'Don't try and escape,' I said, 'because, if you do, what are you going to do? If you try and get back into Cafunfo, probably FAPLA will shoot you. And if you are left out in the bush, there are not many of you who know how to survive, find food and water and so on.'

For myself I would not have been worried; on my own I could probably have made it, particularly as I had had a lot of experience in living rough: but with sixteen Filipinos, not a hope.

What turned our minds to escape was the MIGs. We could see then why UNITA were so keen to get themselves and us and their booty out of town. A squadron of MIG 21s, delta wings, came screeching over Cafunfo about mid-morning, their crews not knowing that the town had been virtually abandoned, bombing and strafing and generally finishing off the destruction that UNITA had begun. Of course FAPLA had been in radio contact with their headquarters; and as soon as headquarters realized the battle was lost, they called up air support and in came the MIGs from Malanje air base. Our feelings were pretty mixed up by then of course. A few hours before we had been working for the government; FAPLA had been defending us, and UNITA was the enemy. Now we were with the UNITA lads, and those MIGs, if they had spotted UNITA, would have blasted us away at the same time. In a way we had switched sides. It was certainly safer to stay with UNITA than to be 'rescued'; we all realized this.

Besides, they were treating us with a bit more respect now. We were sitting down in long grass and skimpy trees, under a bit of cover. A couple of UNITA guys came walking up when we were sitting there and one of them snatched my cap off. I thought, 'Sod that!' and I got up and snatched it back – because if I had lost my hat, I'd have had it. I like the peak over my eyes for protection against the sun. What was interesting was that the bloke didn't do anything. Oh-ho, I thought, and put my hat back on. So now I knew we could stick up for our rights a bit, provided we didn't push it too far. We were dying of hunger and thirst by now, but they would not let us rest for long; they kept pushing us along.

It must have been about 2 o'clock, and I should say we were six miles from Cafunfo, when we heard another plane overhead. We all took cover. At first we thought it was a MIG, but then it circled round and we could hear it touching down on the runway at Cafunfo. The UNITA lads with us became wildly excited. They were all jumping up and down yelling, '*Soviet! Soviet!*' and firing off their AK 47s. But I knew it wasn't a Soviet plane of any sort. I had recognized the sound of the reverse thrust as it landed. Then, a minute or two later, there was a loud explosion on the runway. Christ, I thought, there goes the Hercules bringing in our supplies and spare parts!

That Saturday morning Paul Huggins was the cargomaster on the Hercules. Paul came from Dorking, Surrey. Aged 22, he was an apprentice motor mechanic, but although he had his indentures he hated being a mechanic. He swopped his indentures around because he had four or five different jobs while he was an apprentice. He was one of those lads who could never turn up on time for work, and was a little bit obnoxious at times – and stubborn. Then he started working for another bloke overhauling a boat and he worked on that for about a year. When that came to an end he went on the dole. Paul was spoilt. He had never really had to fend for himself in his teenage years. His character at that time was very unstable, unpredictable. But he was fed up with being on the dole, just oddjobbing.

He was depressed. He was a lad determined to work.

All of a sudden a mate in a pub who worked for Trans-American Airways at Stansted told him there was a vacancy there for a cargomaster. He was down there like a bullet, just on the offchance, and he got it. For him it was a godsend. Trans-American Airways are a big outfit. They operate worldwide, not just in the States but in South America and Africa. They run something like 17 to 18 Hercules, plus DC 8s, and have their fingers in lots of different pies. The pilots are American but they often have British cargomasters because they are half the price. They sent Paul to Ethiopia first. He was about a month or six weeks in Ethiopia, and he admitted that when he saw the devastation there he grew up a bit. At about the beginning of December they transferred him to Angola.

Trans-American Airways were our lifeline in Angola. We were supposed to have something like one convoy a week come through from Luanda, the capital, on the west coast, to Lunda Norte, the diamond-mining province in the north-east – and we are talking of convoys of 150–200 vehicles, bringing petrol, oil, gas, spare parts, supplies. But in fact that year, 1984, maybe only thirteen convoys set out, and when the vehicles arrived in Dundo, the mining operations headquarters near the border with Zaire, they were full of bullet holes, even though they had had massive escorts. When the convoys came through, they had air support, helicopters, armoured cars – the lot. But even so, of perhaps thirteen convoys that set out, maybe nine made it. UNITA were really making it difficult. That road is littered with trucks and débris. There was one 200-vehicle convoy, and nothing got through; everything was destroyed.

So Trans-American Airways contracted to fly in our supplies. What they would do was to bring in a Hercules, which would work for a month and then be changed for another plane while the first one would go back to Germany for servicing. When it was in Angola, the Hercules was in use almost all the time. Trans-American had an excellent record there. They had to fly in all the fuel from Luanda to Dundo, also all our food and all our spare parts. Dundo had a proper asphalt runway with landing lights, so during the nights Trans-American Airways would ferry in the fuel: gas-oil. It was a two-hour trip from Luanda, a four-hour round trip. During the daytime they would fly fuel down to Lucapa and then on to us at Cafunfo. We relied on them entirely because UNITA had cut the road from Malanje to Cafunfo too, and Cafunfo depended entirely on air support. So the fuel had to be continually flown in. Sometimes we would have three days' non-stop production at Cafunfo and other mines and then we would run out of diesel. Then everything would stop, and we would just sit for three or four days until the diesel came through. So Trans-American Airways had a hell of a time. We used to get a flight approximately every ten days, and we relied on them entirely.

As the Hercules was in continual operation, something like 17 hours a day – a long time – it meant that the maintenance of the craft had to be absolutely on the ball. There were three crews to one Hercules, so you had three crews working shifts every day. They comprised three English cargomasters, three captains, three co-pilots, three engineers. That particular Saturday morning Paul Huggins was the cargomaster and the engineer was Al – Al Bongard. It was bad luck on Al; aged 57, he had a paunch and a double chin and was a right physical mess. A mate of his who was normally on the crew went sick, so Al took his place just for that one flight. The captain had checked with Brian Ogilvy, the area manager, the night before; there were no problems at Cafunfo, so they loaded up and flew out from Dundo at about 11 a.m. They were carrying general cargo, medical supplies, spare parts: a load of about 14 tons. It was about a two-hour flight, so, as I said, they were approaching Cafunfo at about 1 o'clock. This of course was about four hours after UNITA had largely pulled out – though not entirely, as soon became clear – and three hours after the government MIGs had blasted the place. But Trans-American knew nothing about that. For some reason no radio message had been sent to Dundo, and at Cafunfo the Hercules always came in hit or miss, with no radio information. If there was a big hole in the runway, they wouldn't worry about it. As far as the captain was concerned, it was just a routine morning and a routine flight.

They were approaching Cafunfo with the tail down just to let us know they were coming in. Jim Taggart, lying hidden in the grass a few hundred yards away, watched them come down, hardly able to believe his eyes. They came over, didn't see anything out of the ordinary – there were no fires or anything else to suggest trouble – and were turning into the final approach when Bill Reed, the co-pilot, and Al saw an explosion like flack about 150 feet below the port wing. But it didn't worry the Captain. 'Probably that's a tracer,' he said. At Dundo when the Hercules was landing at night FAPLA were so trigger-happy that they often let loose a burst of tracer. It was quite a common occurrence. So to see tracer in the daytime didn't mean a lot. The Hercules continued its approach.

Paul was sitting on the cargomaster's seat behind the flight crew when they heard a noise in the back – a banging noise. Al the engineer told Paul to go and have a look. So Paul undid his seatbelt and as he went into the back he heard a ripping noise coming from the front of the aeroplane to the back. He couldn't figure out what it was. He came back to the cockpit to strap himself down for landing and just raised his hands, palms open, to the rest of the crew to show them that he did not know what was wrong. (It was impossible to talk, because of the engine noise.)

As the plane touched down and went into reverse thrust, the big electrical circuit panel behind the cargomaster's seat started exploding, all the fuses banging and the panel pouring out smoke. Al started throwing all the switches off, shutting off the power on the assumption that they had an electrical fault. He was still thinking he had an electrical problem – the same sort of thing had happened before with the lights exploding – when his window caved in on him.

That was just as they were on the ground and taxi-ing to a halt. Paul meanwhile had gone down to the hold to see what the banging had been. He realized what it was then all right. Bullets were pouring through the fuselage and pinging all around him like bees. They had had two Angolan passengers on the plane who knew at once what was happening. They were scrabbling to get out. Al came down from the flight deck, pushed them out of the way and opened the cargo-hold door, and out they ran, like the clappers. He thought they had escaped but later we discovered they had both been killed. Al stepped out of the hatch too, on to the runway. Then suddenly he realized he was being shot at, so he just hurled himself down and lay flat on the ground by the plane as if he were dead.

At that moment a missile of some sort, probably an RPG, hit the nose cone. It blew the nose cone off and smashed all the radar. The cockpit filled with black smoke. The Captain couldn't see anything. He was gagging on the smoke. He forced open the left-hand window in the cockpit, then, though it was only about 18 inches wide by 14 inches long, somehow or other – and he still does not know how he did it – he managed to squeeze himself through and jump out. The trouble was that these Hercules cockpits are high up: it was a drop of nearly 20 feet to the ground. He landed on both his feet, but he smashed them up badly. Then he picked himself up and started walking forward shouting '*Americano, Americano.*'

Meanwhile in the hold Paul was panicking. Bullets were whanging off acetylene cylinders all over the place; and smoke started pouring up from the wheel arches. Paul ran to the cargo hatch and saw Al lying outside on the ground, apparently dead. So he scurried back in again, jumping between the boxes and crates; by this time Bill the co-pilot was down there too. Smoke was pouring up to the ceiling and down again, becoming so thick that it was impossible to breathe, and at the back the cargo burst into flames. Paul was standing beside Bill and Bill just spun round and fell on the floor beside him. Paul couldn't stand it any more. He shook Bill.

'Bill, are you all right?' he said.

There was no answer. Bill had been hit in the throat by a bullet that had come in through the cargo hatch and though Paul did not realize it at the time, Bill was already dead or dying.

By this time the firing seemed to have stopped. Paul ran out of the Hercules, and then, to his amazement, Al got to his feet and ran too, and they both came to a halt about six or seven yards away. UNITA troops were running up to capture them; the lieutenant-colonel had already grabbed hold of the Captain by his wrists and marched him off.

As they looked back, they could see that the no. 2 engine, on the left-hand side, was on fire. The fuel was dropping out of the wing down the side of the aeroplane into the wheel arch. Paul made a move to go back into the plane to drag Bill out – he and Bill had known each other in Ethiopia. But UNITA grabbed hold of him and pulled him away. They dragged them all back, well out of the way. And that was it. The Hercules went up in flames. She didn't explode, just burnt. As for Bill Reed, the co-pilot, his body was burnt. Later on they found his gold wedding ring and two hip bones.

That was the end of Trans-American Airways' operations in Angola. They heard what had happened at once because a Beechcraft with a Swiss crew, a 9-seater, had been coming in to land after the Hercules. The pilot saw the Hercules hit when he was coming in for a low approach, so he made a low pass instead and flew straight back up again. That was it. Trans-American immediately stopped all operations and pulled out.

The first we knew of this incident was at about 4 or 4.30 p.m. when these three palefaces came walking through the bush with a big UNITA escort. UNITA had driven them out of Cafunfo into the bush in one of our Land Rovers, and then made them walk the last couple of miles. Paul was in a bad way because while he was in the aeroplane being shot at, little bits of shrapnel and hot aluminium had buried themselves in his skin. He had something like 35 to 40 punctures, all over the place. Over the next two or three weeks the punctures would turn septic and we would have to squeeze all this aluminium out. He will have some of those scars till he dies.

But Paul was a young bloke and, apart from the shock and the humiliation, we could see he was going to be all right. And of course it reassured him to meet two fellow Britishers (he hardly knew his American colleagues). Al was in a worse state because he was so much older and to look at him you wouldn't have thought he would be up to any physical exertion. But Al never really got perturbed about anything. He was an extremely easy-going character. He could make a joke out of a serious situation, so he was a good morale-booster.

The one who was really in a bad way of course, because of the state of his feet, was the Captain. He had fractured his heels and the balls of his feet. (When, eventually, he got back to the States, he had to have them broken and reset again.) But we soon found that he was a man it was impossible to have much sympathy for. I am not even going to mention the Captain's name in this story, because I don't want to slag him off after all he has been through. But facts are facts, this is as true an account as I can honestly make it, and I have to say truly that despite all we were to go through together none of us at the end was sorry to see the back of this man.

In appearance the Captain was very tall and thin. He was 6 foot, probably 6 foot 1. He was 57, the same age as Al, and he was a physical fitness freak. But when he was stripped off naked he was a pathetic sight. His ribs and hips stuck out. He looked a bit like a Belsen victim. This was his idea of peak physical fitness. It totally baffled us. But that did not worry him. He was a total loner. He said to me many a time: 'I don't need company. I don't need anybody. I don't even need my wife. She is just an asset.'

In the early days when we were talking he would tell us about his wife. He had told her that he was an atheist and that he didn't believe in God, and also that he didn't want any kids. 'Those are the terms you marry me on,' he had said. She married him, and she kept in line with his views just as they had agreed. She was a keep-fit nut like him.

'O.k,' I said, 'I am an atheist. There is no way I can believe in God and this, that and the other. But I don't want to stop anyone else believing what they want to believe. Let everyone believe what they want to believe. If religion does them any good, good luck to them.'

But the Captain said no; if he had his way, he would stop all religion all over the world, burn down the churches and everything.

'You probably had an overdose of the Jews,' I said, knowing that he had emigrated from Germany to the United States after the war.

'They are just animals,' he said. 'They are not worth talking about.' He was a weirdo.

Among Trans-American Airways pilots he was the lowest of the low. When their western airlines branch had gone on strike in America he had been unemployed, and they took him on as a pilot – Trans-American had some vital contracts to keep running. He flew out there as a strike-breaker for them for nine months while the rest of the lads stayed on strike. In Dundo, Angola, Trans-American had a big house where all the crew members lived together. But he never socialized with them; he never even spoke to them, and it didn't bother him a bit.

After the Americans had been brought in to join us under the trees, we were all asked to come one by one to a small group of UNITA men sitting there. They had a notebook in which they took down our names. Then they said, 'Right, we want all your documents and valuables.'

Many Filipinos had wallets with them, and so did the Americans. All I had was the bunch of keys which always hung on my shorts: keys to the house, workshop and offices. The Filipinos had to write their own names down, their ages, nationality, how much money was in their wallets, what currency it was in, and what else was in the wallets. UNITA went through everybody, noting it all down carefully and then everything, money, keys, papers and so on, was confiscated.

Way after the Americans had arrived, it must have been about 7 p.m., just after dark, while we were under these trees, they brought in another Portuguese. This man was unreal. He had a massive beard and straggly hair; he was totally unkempt and he stank like the clappers – a right mess. He was just a layabout. UNITA had found him in the village, in the native quarter, and they made him a prisoner too. As far as we could discover he had been in Angola for 27 years, and I think he had spent about 16 years of that just bumming about, an unemployed yobbo. He was a short guy, about 5 foot 5 or 5 foot 6. He was used to eating with his fingers.

When he was captured by UNITA he didn't seem perturbed at all. Alone of the Portuguese, UNITA showed him no ill feeling because of his nationality. Generally speaking there was bad feeling between the Portuguese and the Angolans. It was surprising how deep it ran. The Portuguese have given the Angolans a rough time: they have occupied their country for over 500 years, and now the Angolans are not going to let them forget it. But this character hadn't been back to Portugal for 27 years. He was a bit of a loudmouth and he could get the UNITA lads going. They laughed at his jokes: I didn't understand any of them personally but I think most of his jokes were aimed at himself or at the Portuguese nation. That is the impression I got. He was always chattering as he was walking. We nicknamed him Bushbunny, because it seemed to suit him.

That night, as it grew darker and darker, UNITA lit up little fires all over the place and began cooking dinner. It was just as well, because we had now been over twelve hours without a drink or any food and were starving as well as thirsty – but lo and behold, they ate everything themselves and gave us nothing but water. There we all were, the full contingent of hostages (though of course we had no way of knowing that ourselves yet), in captivity and about to face a 600-mile trek through the bush, with unknown discomforts and dangers ahead: three Englishmen, two Americans, seventeen Filipinos, three Portuguese foremen and one almost native Portuguese hobo. It was an odd mixture, to say the least. None of us the previous night had had the slightest inkling that we would all be thrown together for this adventure in Africa, and none of us knew what the outcome would be, whether we would make it or not. Of everyone there I suppose I was, in terms of experience, the best prepared – Bushbunny apart, because in his own way he knew how to get around – for what was to follow.

Chapter 2

Before Angola

The greatest difficulty in my life has been that I have always hated routine. There is no way that I could go to work at the same time every morning and go home at the same time every night. I have done it on occasion – when I was working for Merryman at Thurmaston in Leicester, and I had to drive from Groby to Thurmaston. I would pass the same jogger, the same office girl, every day – it was driving me insane. So I used to alter my hours of work, just to avoid this; as I was the foreman, I had the whole shop to myself anyway. I hate routine. I like variety. After being in the army and touring all over the place I have never been able to stay long in one spot.

The army was a good place for me once I had learnt to accept discipline. I think I would have been a difficult person if I had not had to do National Service, probably quite obnoxious in terms of my attitude to work and lack of respect for people.

Take my motorbiking, for instance. When I was a kid I was always the leader of the gang. I had my first motorbike when I was thirteen and I managed to strip it out and get it working again. I have always been interested in mechanics. I was brought up on the outskirts of Leicester. My mates and I always spent our time in Bradgate Park and Switherland and Sherwood – all over the place, out in the countryside. The police caught me driving my motorbike across the fields when I was 14, and charged me with sixteen offences. In those days they took you down to the police station and gave you a right good dogging and kicked you out. I had my backside paddled a few times by the village bobby.

I went to school in Leicester, just an ordinary secondary-modern school, but I left it early to serve my apprenticeship. I was on about £3 a week and really struggling for money. But I was determined to get my apprenticeship done. When I had finished it, I moved down south to a place called Ottershaw, near Woking in Surrey, mainly to get away from Leicester and be nearer my parents, who were then living not far away – my father was a commercial artist and always moving home.

I had known my first wife from when I was 11 or 12. We

seemed to grow up together. She worked in a plastics factory on a plastic-extruding machine: not much of a job, but good money. She used to come down to Ottershaw for weekends. Then we got married, in a registry office, and about a year after that I got called up for the army. This was in 1959, when I was 21.

The discipline was very hard for me to take at first and I spent a lot of time confined to barracks or in the glasshouse. I found it difficult to accept an injustice and just let it ride. For example, one training day we went to a rifle range, about 300 troops in 14 vehicles, at a place called Cerne Abbas (we were stationed at Yeovil in Somerset).

It was absolutely pouring down, and our captain came along and said: 'Right, you four, get out of that truck.' So we got out of the truck and he said: 'Distribute these containers of food among the trucks.'

So we did this and climbed back into our truck.

'No way,' he said. 'You are soaking wet. You can't sit with the other troops.'

So we had to go out and sit in the truck that had brought the containers. Half an hour later he told us to get out and go and collect all the containers again, which we did. Then we loaded them into the truck. He then told us to ride back in that truck, so we bounced along on the top of these containers. We arrived back at the camp, where we were told to unload the containers. So this truck backed up to the kitchen and we started unloading them. Then the captain turned to a sergeant and said: 'Take these four men in with you and get them scrubbing out the containers.'

By this time I was highly tee'd off about the whole thing, because to pick on four men out of 300 and not share the work about a bit was, to me, an injustice.

'You lot can get stuffed,' I said, and I walked off.

I went down to my barracks, got stripped off and went into the showers.

While I was in the shower, four big hairy hands ripped into the shower and ripped me out and I was in the guard room in about two seconds flat; I spent about 28 days there.

That was just one incident out of many that I still remember vividly. It was just bloody-mindedness on my part. Eventually, sitting in the glasshouse contemplating my navel, I thought to myself: 'Here you are, you're 21, and all the other lads are only

18 or 19. You ought to show *more* sense than them at your age instead of less. You have to buckle down to it, my lad, or else you are going to be in the army for 20 years instead of two.'

So I buckled down to it, came through my basic training – it had taken me three months instead of six weeks because of my lack of discipline – and was transferred to Germany: to Hameln, the Pied Piper's town, a very pleasant place. I was in the Royal Army Service Corps. Being a mechanic, I liked driving; it was a bridging company, and within four weeks I was up in what they called the 'heavy' platoon with the ten-ton mammoths.

In BAOR I did exceptionally well. I enjoyed it. There was a lot of swanning around, all over the place, over to Holland and Belgium and back. I was asked to stay on as a regular on four occasions, but I was determined to get out because, though it did a lot for me as regards my general attitude and my work, I knew I could not take that level of discipline all my life. They offered me promotion to sergeant if I would stay on. But I refused because I was on National Service, so they promoted me up to lance-jack instead. I went on orders, got my stripe up, came off orders in my best battledress, then down to the square; it was traditional for everyone to rag you – stamp on your boots, generally scuff you up.

But one lad went too far. He stubbed his cigarette out on the back of my hand – I still have the scar today – and that was it. I got tucked into him and gave him seven bells. We were thumping each other on the floor when I glanced round and saw this pair of glossy boots and creases like razor blades. It was the captain, the second-in-command. The next morning I was on orders again and got bust back down to driver. Right, I thought, that is the end of the dizzy heights of promotion; that is the end of that. No, the army was definitely not the career for me.

However, the army gave me the taste, and the training, for working with heavy plant. When I was demobbed and came back to the UK, the first company I worked for was the Ham River Brick Company in Chertsey, Surrey. When I left Ham River I moved to another company in Ascot, Berkshire, with long-distance road transport. I was with them about two years, driving about all over the place, up and down the country, and I enjoyed that.

But by the end of two years I decided transport was

becoming monotonous. One thing led to another, and I decided to go back to Leicester. I went to work for a heavy plant company called Contract Plant Hire on Barby Road. I ran a mobile workshop for them, repairing heavy plant all over the country. Next I went to work for a much bigger outfit, Merryman at Thurmaston, on 120-ton motor-scrapers, really big plant, and I enjoyed this a great deal. I worked there for about two-and-a-half years. Then we had a big contract on the M6; I couldn't get on with the field foreman, an Irish lad, thick as two short planks, and in the end I jacked it in.

Next I went into a company called CTB, which was laying a gas pipeline from Kingsley to Rugby. I resigned in sympathy with a friend who was dismissed for some misdemeanour. Next I went to C.A. Blackwell's, where I was made foreman within three months. We did the M6 from Crick to Coventry, the M62 in Manchester, the M1 at Sheffield, the M5 at Clevedon in Somerset, the M18 at Doncaster – a lot of motorways. I also worked as a sub-contractor for some of the other big earth-moving companies on the motorways. I really enjoyed touring about.

When I was working on the M5, I was promoted up to Field Plant Manager. This involved a lot of desk work, and I stood this for a year. Then I thought I was losing touch, and I don't like to lose touch. So I resigned. I like to organize and co-ordinate and let other people do the paperwork, under my authority. I enjoy responsibility but I like it at foreman level. In England I was a foreman for five different companies, which suited me. I don't like to go above that level, but I don't like to go below it either.

By the time I was 30 I had moved from Leicester to Groby and bought my own house. The house was derelict when I bought it. It had a demolition order on it, but I managed to get that lifted. I put on a new roof, built an extension on the lounge and the kitchen, and put dormer bedrooms in, all in my spare time. But now that I was 30, my joints were starting to creak and groan because I had been working out in the wet and cold of the British Isles twelve months a year for too many years. It was time for a change.

A Scottish friend of mine, in fact the friend whom I had resigned from CTB in sympathy with, had taken an overseas contract in Ethiopia. He contacted me and asked if I was interested. I was. I filled in all the application forms and went to Caterpillar's training centre in Geneva – Caterpillar is *the* heavy earth-moving machinery outfit – where I passed a mechanical aptitude test. Caterpillar plant is produced by Caterpillar of Illinois, a gigantic operation with dealerships worldwide. We packed the whole family up – wife, two daughters, one son, myself – and flew out to Ethiopia in early 1971.

I spent three-and-a-half years in Ethiopia, and of that three-and-a-half years I probably spent three living in a tent. I was with the same guy all the time, my mechanic, Wolde Tekle, an Eritrean, roaming all over the place on field service. We had a high-powered radio and I was in contact with the head office every day, or every time I needed to know new locations. My job was to service Caterpillar machines for a Caterpillar dealer. I had been working with Caterpillar machines on all the motorway programmes in the UK but this was different; if you work for a dealer you have to be on the ball, particularly overseas.

Wolde Tekle spoke three tribal languages, and he knew the country. Ethiopians are very proud people but, because the economic climate in Ethiopia is such a disaster, once they do get a job they will do anything to hang on to that job, absolutely anything; but you can't rub their noses in it, because of their pride. I like the Ethiopian people. Once you find out their characteristics they are easy to get on with. There were a few obnoxious characters but generally the Ethiopians were friendlier than most of the nationalities I have worked with, before or since. I got friendly with many black farm managers and governors of little townships and small communities all over the country.

The first year-and-a-half we were all over Ethiopia. Then I was subcontracted to a German company that was making a road from Awash on the railway line across the Danakil desert to join up with the road coming from Assab on the Red Sea. This was about 1973, when the drought was at its worst. The political climate had started to change too. There were student riots in Addis Ababa and Asmara. But that hardly affected me, as I was based in the Danakil desert. I would probably work there a month, then go off on another job, probably two or three days or a week at a time, then come back and continue.

There were no other whites around in the Danakil desert, other than me and a few Germans, and because I got so friendly with the Danakils I was invited to some quite extraordinary celebrations and ceremonies which perhaps no white man has ever seen before. They have a reputation for cruelty, the Danakils, and for having mutilated more explorers than any other tribe in Africa. One bloke I met, Mohammed Bijanga, a leader of the Bate clan, had a black string around his neck with various knobs along it.

'What are those things around your neck?' I asked him.

'They are testicles,' he said.

'I beg your pardon?'

'That is the way we prove that we are warriors. When we kill a man, we cut his testicles off, then we dry them and hang them round our necks.'

I was thunderstruck. I counted seven pairs there and one sort of whitish pair, so I said: 'Is that white?'

'Yes.'

'Exactly who is that, then?'

'That is an Italian from the Mussolini war.'

'I just hope I don't get mine hanging around anybody's neck,' I said; and he laughed heartily. I wasn't too sure if I really appreciated that laugh of his.

Meanwhile, unbeknown to me, my wife was having an affair with an American who was stationed in Addis Ababa – I had found a house for the family there three weeks after our arrival, and the children were at the French Lycée in Addis. I came back, eventually found out and there was a big punch-up. I had done two years by that time, so I went home on leave with the children. But my wife abandoned us all and took herself off to live with her American boyfriend. There I was, on my tod, left in Groby with three kids. I didn't quite know what to do. Fortunately my 21-year-old sister, Yvonne, who was still single, volunteered to come and live in my house and look after the kids; they would remain in England, with my mother dropping in every day, while I went back to work abroad and sent money for the expenses. We settled all the arrangements and off I flew, back to Ethiopia. Things were really beginning to hot up there now. This was mid-1974, and I remember the runway at Addis airport was blocked; I was delayed 14 hours. But I got back safely, and I took another, smaller, house in Addis, on the southern outskirts, on the Nazareth Road.

My first assignment was in the mountains in the south, at a

place called Ginir. The rainy season had begun. We were driving up to Ginir, Wolde Tekle and myself, through a torrential rainstorm. It was about 7 or 8 at night, and we saw in the headlights a body being washed down the side of the road. It sort of waved at us as it went past, so I stopped, rushed back down the road and dragged this body out of the water. It was a young girl aged about 17 or 18, very much alive, and all she had on was a pair of pants and one sandal.

Wolde and I got her into the jeep, wrapped her in a blanket and drove on up into Ginir. Ginir is just a primitive little town; there is no hotel or anything like that. So we pitched our tent and she slept in the back of the pick-up. We fixed a tarpaulin over it so she was nice and dry.

In the morning I gave her one of my workshirts to wear and she started cooking for us, making herself useful, washing our clothes. I could see that she would attach herself to us unless we were careful, particularly when we found out that she was from the north, from Gojjam. She explained that she had come down to see relatives but she had not been able to find them. She had run out of money. When she had tried to wade across this torrent, she got caught and washed down, while all her clothes were ripped off her; that was when we had spotted her.

That very day I got a radio message telling me I was wanted urgently in the Ogaden and the office sent a Cessna down to the airstrip at Ginir to pick me up. I went myself, leaving Wolde and the jeep and the girl behind. I was three weeks in the Ogaden repairing various bits of plant for Texaco and then they flew me back down to Ginir. The girl was still there, so I said: 'Scarper! Hop it!' By this time I could speak Amharic fluently.

'No,' she said, 'I want a lift to Addis Ababa.'

That was where my next appointment was, so off we went to Addis. Wolde took her to his house (he had a wife and two kids) and put her up.

The next assignment was in Assab up on the Red Sea, in Eritrea. We loaded the jeep up on Saturday and on Monday morning before dawn off we went to Assab. We drove down through Awash and then headed north across the Danakil desert road, the new road I had been working on which was now about to open. About four hours later we stopped to have breakfast. Up with the tarpaulin and, blow me, there was the girl sitting in the back, as pleased as punch. Well, I wasn't going back to Addis and I could hardly put her out in the middle of the desert, especially with the Danakils at large, so there was no choice really. I took her to Assab.

We trailed around Assab for about a month; one thing led to another, and we ended up sleeping together. She was a real bush girl. She couldn't eat with a knife and fork, but she was very intelligent. When we got back to Addis she moved into my house and within three months she was eating with a knife and fork and so on. Her name was Mulu Belude. (A girl has two names, a daily name and a feminine name, and that was her daily name. Her feminine name was Tsahai – to me she was Tsahai.) I used to give her 500 Ethiopian dollars a month. I opened a bank account for her and sent her to school. She was very quick; she was soon speaking English with me and my friends.

Meanwhile the revolution, which had begun fairly mildly with a taxi drivers' strike in February, was coming to its climax. The Emperor was still in control, just, but the soldiers were making demands and mutinying left, right and centre. The generals couldn't control them, and law and order were breaking down. I had orders to take a big Caterpillar machine, a grader, to a plantation run by the British company Mitchell Cotts, down past Nazareth. Wolde Tekle had gone on ahead of me driving the grader, and I caught up with him in the jeep just as he was driving through Nazareth. There were black palls of smoke all over the place, so I knew there was trouble looming.

All of a sudden a big brick came flying through the windscreen and hit me in the chest. It took the windscreen out and then other bricks followed from all directions, taking the side windows out. I peered through the smoke, and saw rioters closing in. Ethiopians get really hysterical when they are worked up, and I realized that if I stopped I would be in big trouble.

I had this Smith and Wesson .38 in a shoulder holster under my jean jacket. I pulled this out and flourished it through the hole where the windscreen had been and fired two rounds in the air. That was it. The place cleared: within seconds there wasn't a soul in sight. Wolde meanwhile had driven straight on through, without any problem. But ahead there was a bus lying on its side, on fire and blocking the road. Wolde had driven down into the ditch and up round it. But I couldn't get past. The mob was closing up again behind me and more rioters were moving around in front. So I went smack into reverse and swung the jeep round, holding the revolver where everyone could see it, and they parted and let me through, shouting and all that, but not a brick thrown. But if I had not had that Smith & Wesson there, I hate to think what would have become of me.

That night, about 11 p.m., I left Addis Ababa again and drove through Nazareth, which was all quiet. I hadn't been worried about Wolde because he was a man of many means, and I knew that once he had passed Nazareth he would never be stuck. Indeed I caught up with him again in Awash and we carried on and that was the end of that. We were away for about two months. When we came back there were checkpoints everywhere on the roads leading into the capital. It took us about two hours to get through all these checkpoints. Inside Addis there were police and army all over the place.

Next day I went into the office and they told me I would be a demonstrator driver on some new equipment that had come in. So the following day I went out to the old airport to start preparing the ground for the demonstration. Wolde and I were driving machines around, and Tsahai was sitting in my car.

A black Mercedes drove up, escorted by two police outriders, and came to a stop beside my car. I was about 100 yards away and I could see the police telling Tsahai to get out and come round to the Mercedes. I could see her bowing and nodding her head there; the man inside gave her a dollar, then she went back to my car. Then they waved me over.

It was the Emperor. He was driving around distributing dollars personally in a forlorn attempt to stave off the revolution. Not that he offered me one. He simply asked me what I was doing. I told him, and he wished me all the best. Then they called Wolde over. I was standing near my car, and could hear everything.

'What part of Ethiopia are you from?' asked the Emperor.

'Eritrea, Your Majesty,' said Wolde.

'Do not say any more,' said the Emperor. 'Just go.' So Wolde bowed, and came and stood beside me, and the door closed, and the Emperor drove off. Four days later he was dethroned.

I had a lot of respect for Haile Selassie – though he didn't care for the Eritreans. Of course, by this time he was a very old man, and a rather pathetic one.

It was a hard life for his people. Ethiopia was a very poor country and there was corruption among those of high rank. But further down, in the police force and the civil service, it was not as corrupt as other parts of Africa. I am not politically minded and I do not like to get involved in politics, but it was sad to see Haile Selassie go. The place degenerated into complete turmoil after the Emperor was dethroned.

About ten weeks later, on what they called 'Bloody Saturday', 23 November 1974, they brought a lot of my old acquaintances, including governors, to Addis Ababa, and executed them together with many generals and 21 ministers. That was a sad day. Generally there were brutalities going on in little corners all over the place. The Eritreans were having a rough time. There was drought and famine all around the Dessie plateau, and in Wollo to the north. A lot of tribesmen would come down into the capital, sleeping on the pavements at night. In the morning the army trucks would go round collecting all the corpses.

We were sent up to Dessie for the goverment with two D6 bulldozers, passing many little villages. There were some pathetic sights. We stopped just outside a small village for lunch, and Wolde made me corned beef sandwiches. I felt a right heel eating these sandwiches with kids gathered all around and an eyeball on every move I made. So I broke the sandwiches in halves and gave out half each, and within twenty minutes a little girl – she must have been about 3 or 4 – went into convulsions. Half an hour later she was dead. I don't know whether the sandwich killed her or what it was, her stomach was so blown out.

Even then, even when they were starving, the Ethiopians were still fanatically religious. I have never been religious really. I was indifferent – no real reason, religion just never interested me. If I had had the choice of standing inside a church or standing outside it, I would have stood outside. But I think this time round Dessie was the beginning of my becoming a real atheist. Those Ethiopians – they were all Christians in the highlands – truly believed that God would help them. It was quite pathetic.

Back in Addis it became very difficult at work. The people had become more aggressive – they did not have to be so submissive any longer, and they were showing it. We were sent down to

Nazareth again, to repair a small generator that some hooligan had damaged. Coming back in the evening we stopped at a checkpoint, just a bar across the road; as we got out, for no reason at all the soldiers attacked us.

They hit me in the bottom of the spine with rifle butts, and that put me on my knees. Then one of them hit me on the side of my neck, and I went down on my side. Then they started kicking me in the ribs. They rough-handled me but they really beat up Wolde. Cuts and bruises apart, he lost two teeth, split an eardrum, had two broken ribs and a crushed big toe. They just threw us into the ditch. Then they ransacked the car – I always carried about $300 worth of food, mainly tinned stuff – and pushed the car into the ditch too. There was no particular reason for it all – that was the baffling part.

For about two hours I just lay in that ditch. Then I got the first-aid kit out and started plastering Wolde together again. It was about 10 p.m. by the time we had dug the muck out and made a ramp and got the car back on to the road again. The barrier was completely deserted. I drove Wolde to the hospital, but the place was full and they refused to treat him. I had to take him to my own private doctor, a Greek, and he plastered him up.

By this time I was seriously thinking of getting out of the country. Next morning the general manager called us into his office – I turned up limping – and he told us that those that wanted to go could go; those who wanted to stay could stay. There were only six of us by this time, and two left within 24 hours.

But I decided to stay. That was a mistake, because on my next trip, to Bahardar in Gojjam, the army threw me and my mechanic – not Wolde, he was still in plaster – into jail, because we did not have the right spare for their engine. After two days they let us out – and this time I was o.k. apart from a split eyebrow. It's getting a bit rough now, I thought. This is the time to pull out. But I had to face one more jail stint two weeks later – for, of all things, taking a photograph of the French school where my daughters had been. It was forbidden to take photographs in Addis at that time, as I found out too late. After I had taken it I was arrested and taken to No. 6 jail for the night. My camera was destroyed and I was asked to leave. I took the next London flight and left everything.

I never saw Tsahai or Wolde again. Tsahai made it back to

Gojjam, I heard, and she was quite rich compared to when she had left, with money in the bank and so on. But I heard later that she died in a student demonstration in Gojjam. I also heard that Wolde Tekle was killed in Addis, along with his brother, wife, daughter and son, maybe because they were Eritreans.

I was a bit cheesed off when I came back to the UK because I had lost everything. I had no job and no wife. But the German company which I had been subcontracted to for the work on the road through the Danakil desert offered me a contract as field area foreman in Oman.

I spent nearly two years in Oman, with leave every six months. I enjoyed Oman, and I like the Omani people – as Arabs, they are the best Arabs I have ever met. And they are very good workers.

It was a very interesting, straightforward contract, though we did have some guerrilla threats and one of our guides was killed in a vehicle which hit a landmine. We had our camp just below the famous Green Mountain, the Jebel Akhbar that the SAS went over, and which goes straight up for 4000 feet. We spent many weekends in the mountains; they are more copper-coloured than green, really. We were working about 200 miles north of Muscat, the capital, so we were very isolated. But occasionally we went down to the coast; the beaches and the sea are fantastic, with some of the best coral I have seen, better than Mombasa. I was on bachelor status, though I was courting between leaves. I met my second wife then, though in fact I had known her from when she was a kid.

I was the only non-German European there working for this German company. There were 26 Germans and myself, and I learnt their language. Omanis apart, I had a crew of 40 Pakistanis and I got good results out of my crew because I treated them better than the Germans did. The Germans are very harsh and demanding – which I like, as long as they don't make demands on me. At the end of the contract, I agreed to overhaul the machinery that the company brought back, and I went out to Germany to do it. I spent seven months there, on the Rhine, on the Dutch border, as *Verkstadtmeister*, workshop foreman, overhauling this equipment for Nigeria. In between, my divorce had come through and I had married Lynn.

We took the equipment down to Bremerhaven and loaded

it, and then I went off to Nigeria. Lynn came out six months later with two of my children by my first wife and her daughter. In all I spent five-and-a-half years in Nigeria working on various contracts, mainly in the centre and north. During the last two-and-a-half years the children were back in England at boarding school while I stayed in Nigeria continuously without taking any leave. That was a mistake. Nigeria takes a lot out of you because of the climate and the Muslims and all the aggressive attitudes. Though I liked the country people and I had some good mechanics and welders in my workshop, the aggro was savage – worse than in any other country I have ever been in. My nerves were going. It came to the point where I would go into the workshop and bawl at one of the mechanics for nothing. Then I would come back into the office and I would think, 'Was that necessary? Why did I dog him?'

'Things are getting on top of me,' I thought. 'I am starting to crack up, I need to get away.' I had not had a good leave after Ethiopia or Oman or during Nigeria. What was more, I had lost contact with the kids. It was about time I went back and spent some time in the UK. I must have been totally obnoxious at work in Nigeria because I would tell the boss to piss off and bury his head in the sand, yet they still put up with me. I resigned about eleven times during that last year. But this time I meant it. So I wrote this long letter of resignation explaining why I needed at least a year off. They agreed, and I resigned. I did not have any feelings at all, one way or the other, on leaving Nigeria.

But within three weeks of being back in England I was totally bored. The trouble was that I had a lot of money in the bank, about £40–45,000, not doing anything, just getting a bit of interest. I knew I could live on it for five to ten years without bothering to work, and that was a bad thing for me because I need pressure to keep me in line.

I decided to sell the house at Groby and I found another house at Burton-on-the-Wolds. It was only about seventeen years old but very neglected, so we ripped the place apart and spent every day there working on it. Lynn and I would work like dogs, never missing a single day, except Christmas Day and Boxing Day. I thoroughly enjoyed it. When I have a project such as renovating a house, I wake up as soon as I have had enough sleep – that could be at 3 a.m. – get up and get cracking. It took us three-quarters of an hour to travel from

Groby to Burton-on-the-Wolds and we were always there by 7 a.m. It was sometimes 9 or 10 p.m. before we got back, dog-tired but happy.

Lynn is a grafter and we work well together. We spent a year-and-a-half on this place and we never had a serious argument. We did everything except the plastering, including the brickwork and the construction – the lot. It really relaxed me. By the time it was done, instead of having £40,000 in the bank I owed the bank about that amout. *Now* I need a job, I thought. So I rang the German company back up again. But they were in dire straits. They had collapsed in Nigeria, they had collapsed in Peru, in the Yemen, in Iraq. They had nothing for me.

So I had to hunt around a bit. There is a trade newspaper that comes out every week, *Construction News*, and in it I saw an advertisement offering a contract in Central Africa. Where in Central Africa, I wondered? But it was with a firm that was a big Caterpillar dealer, a firm called Intraco, so I went up to the interview.

The man who interviewed me in London was a West German called Hilinger. He runs Intraco's Angolan operation. He is a big guy, an overpowering guy: when he walks into a room he becomes the centre of attention and he can hold it. When he shakes hands with you, your hand vanishes in his. He is very direct and he doesn't like asshole creepers, to put it bluntly. When he wants an answer to a question he wants the truth. I am direct myself in that sense. He is a good talker. I have to admire the guy because he speaks German, Spanish and Italian and his Portuguese is fluent, not a hit-and-miss job. He speaks English with an American accent. 'You are a bit old at 44, no, 45, for this type of thing,' he said to me. It was true. It is getting on a bit for overseas, for an expatriate contract. 'But we do need some elderly experienced people over there.'

And that was how I found myself leaving England to work for Intraco out in Angola, going back to Africa once more.

Chapter 3

Lunda Norte, the Diamond Province

It did not worry me at all that Angola was ruled by a Marxist government. As I have said before, politics, like religion, leave me indifferent, though I admire Maggie Thatcher. But I have never voted in my life and from my point of view it did not make any difference what kind of a government it was in Angola. I have to admit I was there for the money. It was a dollar contract, a hard-currency contract, and there are not many of those about. Usually they are local-currency contracts. In any case I had survived five-and-a-half years of aggro in Nigeria and three-and-a-half years of living rough in Ethiopia before that, with a revolution thrown in, so I thought I could survive whatever came up in Angola. And, as it happens, I was right. I could – and I did.

Besides, compared to Ethiopia and Nigeria, and even Oman, Angola was very placid, the most placid country I have ever been in. At first, on arrival, I thought Angola was badly organized – total, utter confusion. It was July 1983 when I arrived, and the country had become independent in November 1975, so they had had almost eight years to get it sorted out. At first I thought they had failed abysmally. Then they flew us up from the capital, Luanda, to the diamond-mining province, Lunda Norte, and I had to change my mind.

The first thing that struck me was the security. Anyone flying from Luanda to Dundo, the internal airport for Lunda Norte, had to have a special permit. The DSD, the security lads, would check your papers and baggage there. Then to move from Dundo to any other area in the province another permit had to be obtained. Without this permit there was no way anyone could travel. I was sent down from Dundo to Andrada, and I had to have a permit for that. Andrada was the main workshop, a massive complex, one of the best African workshops I have seen, and I have seen some. There wasn't much they couldn't do there. The machine shop was unreal. That was the main stores, main workshop, main everything. There are mines around but Andrada was mostly maintenance. Then Duncan Angus, the project manager at Andrada, told me I was to be area foreman at Lucapa. So off to Lucapa we went.

Lucapa was about 100 miles away, and I arrived there on 15 July 1983. They had given us a little lecture with the map of Angola on the wall, saying there was some terrorist activity in the south and that inside the diamond-mining area the previous December terrorists had hit the Cuilo bridge, which Intraco had just rebuilt. But that had been six months earlier, and since then there had been no trouble in our area. As far as UNITA went, it stayed quiet till the end of 1983. It took me a little while to settle in and understand what all the security was about.

They dumped me in Lucapa. Of course, I did not speak Portuguese. That was my big handicap, as everyone was speaking Portuguese. They more or less said: 'This is Lucapa. That is your house. This is your office. That is your workshop. There are some of the people. The others are out on site but you will meet them later. We'll see you when we see you. Bye.'

So I was left there in the middle of nowhere. It took me about three months to get into that job, find out all the nooks and crannies and assess the people and so on. But it did not take me anything like that long to find out about the reasons for the security. It was all because of the diamond-smuggling.

They first discovered diamonds in that part of Angola way back in 1912, and now it is one of the richest seams in the world. The diamonds there are thought to be almost inexhaustible. The Portuguese were in control then, of course, and five years later they set up Diamang – the Companhia de Diamantes de Angola; they call it Diamang for short, and the Angolan government now owns 77 per cent of it.

Diamang became a sort of a state within a state. It had its own police force, its own armoured cars, schools, hospitals; it ran the agriculture – everything. The towns were company towns, just set up for the mining. Dundo on the border with Zaire – it was the Belgian Congo previously, of course – was the biggest; that was the capital, about 30,000 people, with all the bigwigs and 5,000-strong FAPLA forces to protect them. Then there were the mining towns proper, near the riverbeds and mines: Lucapa, Andrada and last of all Cafunfo, built in 1955: those three. Even when what they now call the War of Liberation began in 1960, it didn't much affect this area. There was fighting all over the country, the Portuguese against the three independence movements, and sometimes, even then, the three independence movements against each other, but Lunda Norte was so remote and so sparsely populated that the fighting hardly affected it at all.

Though production did fall in the last four years before independence, from 1970 to 1974, it still came to 2 million carats a year. But what really finished it off was the arrival of independence, on 11 November 1975, upon which the Portuguese pulled out. There had been about 350,000 of them in the country and after independence only about 30,000 stayed on, less than one in ten. The whole place relapsed into utter chaos. The Portuguese hadn't trained anyone, even for semi-skilled jobs; they had done it all themselves – they were the mechanics, engineers, drivers, everything. So when the Angolans were left to run the mines themselves, it was catastrophic. They nationalized Diamang, of course, which didn't help, and in any case they had to rely on De Beers to market their diamonds as before. De Beers controls over 80 per cent of the world market in uncut diamonds, and sets all the prices and so on. So although they were black Marxists, there was no way they could get out of the grip of De Beers, which is white South African and totally capitalist. It was an odd set-up really.

In November 1977 the Angolan President Agostinho Neto – he's dead now – visited Diamang and gave them a right good piece of his mind because production had fallen to something unbelievable, and told them they would have to call in foreign technicians to run the mines for them. So, early the following year, the MATS people came in.

MATS stands for Mining and Technical Services Ltd. It is incorporated in Liechtenstein but in fact it is a De Beers operation, and its main office, in London, backs on to the De Beers fortress in Holborn Circus. MATS was given the contract to run the mines for Diamang, and brought in about 60 expatriates to manage the 17,000 black workers who actually did the manual work, the mining, throughout the concession. They were mainly British, like John MacMichael. John had kept his British citizenship, even though he had emigrated to South Africa. He needed a British passport, because with South African citizenship he wouldn't have been able to get a job in a black country. But he was very South African in his attitude. He was a mining engineer. He had been working in a place called Western Deep, one of the deepest gold mines on the

Rand, looking after all the equipment. One of the mining bosses in the same mine became a great mate of his – he was Afrikaans. Something like five years after John had made friends with this bloke he met his daughter. One thing led to another, and they married. So he was married to a beautiful Afrikaans girl and living in Cape Town; they had only been married a year or so when he came out to Angola. But one thing he did say was that he was thinking of leaving South Africa because he reckoned there was going to be a bloodbath there between the blacks and the whites. That was one reason why he came out to Angola for MATS, to get a bit of experience working outside South Africa. He was planning to take a trip to America and have a look at jobs there; he had had a few offers.

MATS had managed to get the mines working properly again, and production up – though it was never up as high as it had been before independence. But the main problem was the smuggling. They reckoned that between 1981 and 1983 (when I arrived) they had lost over a third of the production in smuggling. The main job of the DSD, Diamang's special police force, is to stop the smuggling. They have almost total powers – and an impossible job.

The *kamanguistos*, the diamond contraband dealers, used to come in mainly across the border from Zaire. The DSD would wait till they had bought up everything and were heading back, then they would grab them with a pocketful of diamonds. They stopped one lad at a checkpoint near the frontier and got something like 70 carats of diamonds off him, which at 200 dollars a carat is a lot of money for a black worker.

The mine-workers were really very badly paid; they were earning next to nothing. The Angolan workforce was a total disaster and if the mines had been relying totally on Angolans nothing would ever have got done. When expatriates arrive in Angola they are told by the bosses not to expect more than 20 per cent productivity from the Angolans. You took notice of that, and it was true. The reason was that the salaries were not worth having and they had nothing to work for. That was why they were ready to take a risk, even though for a black it meant five years in jail. The DSD was on duty twenty-four hours a day, with roving patrols as well as checkpoints. If you saw a diamond on the floor you wouldn't pick it up, you would just walk round it: you had to be that careful. You didn't know where the DSD people were. They could be sitting in a tree a mile away with a telescope or binoculars. You just didn't know who was watching you at any time.

Fortunately they did not bother with the British very much, because even if the British do steal a diamond, there is not much they can do with it. In England it is impossible to sell uncut diamonds legally, unless you are really in the know. In any case an Englishman, even if he is only suspected of stealing, loses his job. The company is not interested in keeping anyone under suspicion because this just means trouble for it. If an employee were caught with a diamond and he did get away, he would never get another job in Angola. I heard about one English lad who was just sitting on a gravel tip, idly throwing stones – and was arrested and expelled within three weeks. That was understandable because another, doing the same, picked a stone up which turned out to be a monster diamond. He handed it into the DSD who took it to Andrada where it was valued at about $½ million. The DSD knew it could more or less trust the English expatriates, so we could go virtually where we liked. We could go into the treatment plants, stand at the end of the cyclone and see the diamonds bouncing down the conveyor belt. It was all locked in and under high security, but we could watch through a grille. It gave you a funny feeling, seeing these diamonds, especially when the sun was shining. At the end of a week there would probably be about a briefcase-full of diamonds out of 250,000 cubic metres of gravel sifted. As you can imagine, the expense of getting the diamonds out of the earth is phenomenal.

I soon learnt that the DSD was corruptible. Cigarettes they just do not have: they are in very short supply throughout the diamond-mining area. Nobody has a cigarette, so everybody is always scrounging. When we were on a flight from Lucapa or Cafunfo, for instance, we would come into Dundo, take our bags into a small room for checking and just leave a packet of cigarettes on top. That would be it: we would be cleared.

The chief of the DSD, Selgado, was a character we had to be very careful of. We had to treat him with complete respect and keep giving him the odd case of beer or carton of cigarettes. He was the top dog in the realm of law and order. He spoke a little bit of English and was quite a pleasant guy. I liked him. He was all right and very direct – probably that is why he got the job.

He had lots of fiddles going, not corruption with money but with furniture, carpets, plumbing, electrical fittings and so on. If we wanted anything done, we had to add a sweetener in kind.

The security police were hard on the Portuguese though (there must have been about 100 Portuguese working for MATS or Intraco), the reason being that it is not illegal to sell uncut diamonds in Portugal. The DSD for some reason got on to one Portuguese in Dundo: they stripped his house, and behind the power sockets on the wall they found five stones – three diamonds and two quartz (the quartz look very much like diamonds: only when you look at them with a glass can you see they are not). They took him away and jailed him. He has been in jail now for about three years without yet standing trial. He has no chance of escape. So that is the end of him. I heard his wife had to become a prostitute to earn money for herself and the kids.

But of course the people the DSD was really after were the Angolans. The Angolans knew this, and that was why we could never carry any Angolans on our transport. If the DSD stopped an Intraco jeep, say, at a checkpoint and there were Angolans on it who had diamonds on them, they would just push the stones down behind the seat or drop them on the floor. Then, if the DSD found them, that was it, bye-bye, the driver would be sent off to jail because it was his car – no argument. We had to refuse absolutely to carry any Angolan people anywhere. In Lucapa, where we had thirteen or fourteen vehicles, I put a notice up on the board: 'Nobody carries passengers of any description unless he works for Intraco.' So we were accused of being racist. I tried to explain why we were doing it. Then the response was: 'You are saying that we black people are thieves then.' Whatever we did, we were wrong.

One night, at a mine called Mufutu, I was driving home rather late at about 9 p.m. It was pitch black, and I could hear this firing going on, AK 47s, grenades exploding, flashes in the night sky . . . It was like a mini-war. I backed up out of the way and switched my lights off. A troop of heavily armed guys came out on to the road, got lined up and marched off. So I sat there for about an hour waiting for them to scarper because I could not be sure who it was. It might have been UNITA. Next morning I asked one of the DSD lads they called Black Bob, 'What was going on down at Mufutu last night? Was it you lot?'

'Yes,' he said. 'Some illegal diamond-diggers, just boys, 15 or 16 years old, they came to sift this sand through for diamond flakes in the river-bed.'

Somebody had spotted them and warned the DSD, and the DSD had laid an ambush for them in the bush. There were fourteen DSD and three of these young lads, and when they came out of the river-bed, the DSD just let rip with everything they had – they were carrying four grenades and 32 rounds each. That was how serious it was for the Angolans if they were caught or trapped, though one of the boys on this occasion apparently dived back in the river and saved his skin.

In order to extract the diamonds, they would even go as far as diverting the course of a river: that was what all the heavy machinery and plant was needed for, changing the course of the Cuango river. Afterwards we closed the river off and opened the river-bed. In the case of the mines in the Lucapa area, they had 25–30 feet of overburden to get through before the diamond gravel was reached. But at Cafunfo it was just a question of whacking the topsoil off, two or three inches. There was one river-bed I remember near Cafunfo containing vast riches. In about 300 yards of river-bed there were two or three hundred pockets of diamonds. The diamonds had washed down the channel, soft volcanic lava rock – then got caught in a little dip, started rotating, cut into the stone and made big pockets, anything up to 15 or 20 feet deep, 4–5 feet in diameter – though funnily enough, sometimes the neck of a pocket is only about 6 inches across, and the pocket bells out underneath. I was told that one hole they dug yielded something like 14,000 carats, at $200 a carat. In the lads went, down with their buckets, shovelled up the gravel, then the crane lifted them up and they tipped the diamond gravel on to the bank. This pile was so rich that the diamonds could be seen sparkling and the foremen were pushing them in with pencils just to try and hide them. Then the DSD would be called down and the men would sit on the top of these piles, AK 47s at the ready.

However, there are ways in which the workers can get their hands on a diamond. Up there in the mining area when the topsoil has been stripped down – say at 5 a.m., just before dawn – they wait for the sun to come up. When it is just up and it gets to a certain angle, they lie flat on their stomachs with their eyes as near as possible to ground level. When the sun hits the diamonds the light is reflected and will catch the eye.

Keeping an eye fixed on the gleaming stone, they say to another lad who they have with them, 'Right, three feet forwards, another foot, 6 inches sideways,' and so on, until he puts his finger on it and can pick the diamond up. To stand up and try to spot diamonds from above is physically impossible. These surface diamonds can sometimes be 6- or 7-carat, so for an Angolan worker, if he is prepared to take the risk and can sell the diamond quickly to a *kamanguisto*, there is a lot of money to be made – a fortune.

At about the beginning of 1984 things started hotting up; at first there were just minor incidents, involving landmines and so on. UNITA were gradually infiltrating their people in the north. I came home that February on leave – they had brought a temporary foreman out to take my place at Lucapa – and while I was sitting at home in Burton-on-the-Wolds watching television I heard that UNITA had attacked and destroyed Cafunfo. It was a shock seeing it all from England on the box, an incident that was remote to everyone else, just something that happened in Africa, but for me something that affected me closely.

When I went back to Angola, I had to report first of all, as usual, to the main workshops at Andrada. 'Have a couple of days here just knocking about,' the project manager Duncan Angus said to me, 'because I want to talk to you about something.'

'Hello, hello,' I said to myself, 'what's all this then?'

After a couple of days' wandering around I went in to see him:

'Let's have it,' I said. 'What are we hanging about for?'

'Well,' he said, 'Shaun, the lad who was brought in to replace you, is not doing a bad job at Lucapa, so I thought we might leave him there. But we need a volunteer to go to Cafunfo. Would you go?'

That is what I had guessed he was going to ask. That had been my first thought. So, as I had already thought about the problem, I said, 'Yes, o.k., I'll go.'

The attack had put Cafunfo totally out of action; it was now deserted.

'We'll have to wait till things get sorted out and quieten down,' he said, 'and then we'll go back in.' He meant till FAPLA had made sure that the UNITA troops who had carried out the assault were well away, out of the whole diamond-mining area. 'In the meantime, just knock around.'

By the end of April I was getting really fed up with 'just knocking around', filling in on other people's jobs or sitting watching videos day after day. So I went to Duncan Angus and said: 'You will have to sort something out or I'm off. I can't stand much more of this.'

'I will see what I can do and try and push it along a bit more,' he promised.

He did; and so on about 12 May we flew into Cafunfo – myself and three Filipinos: two motor mechanics and one electrician. The flight down was terrible. The Portuguese pilot was excellent, but it was raining and there was low cloud and we were in what we called a flying Portacabin – it looked just like one of those portable huts with two wings stuck on. He could not find his way through. In the end he saw a hole in the clouds and dived through it, just like a kamikaze pilot, and all of a sudden the ground was below us and he was scraping the treetops. Once he had found the river, that was o.k., he just followed the river along. But we could not get a view of Cafunfo at all because of the low cloud and teeming rain.

Once we had landed we walked around Cafunfo, aghast. It was devastated. There were power cables hanging down naked, houses had been blown up and, apart from the FAPLA garrison that had moved back in (about 300 lads), the place was still almost deserted. In normal times 2,500 black workers were employed there, but lots of them were still hiding in the bush with their families.

They lived in 'Tin City', the workers, a huddle of tin shacks on the side of the town proper. Cafunfo was only a small place but it was a real company town, built by Diamang thirty years ago when they first started to mine diamonds in the area, with a company food store, cinema, offices, carpenter's shop and so on. There had been about 30 expatriates living there, so there were about eight expatriate houses in the compound, and various other houses for the black upper management, normally with water, electricity and so on laid on. This was quite different from 'Tin City'; it was quite another story for the upper black management in terms of living conditions.

At the workshop we had been told that we would find a convoy lined up, quite a lot of vehicles and equipment, which had been preparing to leave for Andrada when UNITA struck.

We found it all right, or about half of it, but it was in a terrible condition, with bullets through the radiators, tyres and fuel tanks, lights smashed – a right mess. But it could be repaired, and that was the primary job Duncan Angus had given us: to repair it and put it on the road, and drive it up to Lucapa.

The Filipinos and I worked on these vehicles every day. But the system was that the 'Portacabin' would fly us out from Dundo every morning at 6 a.m. and arrive back at 5 p.m. So what with two hours' flying each way, by the time we had it all sorted out there were only about two hours left for doing the work. So I said to Duncan Angus: 'This is ridiculous. Better if we take some camping gear down and we camp in Cafunfo.' (The houses were still all smashed up and uninhabitable.)

'It's up to you,' he said.

So off we went, and within about a week we had nailed all this lot together. The Angolan mechanics that were working in Cafunfo for Diamang had come drifting back in when they saw the workshop functioning again. There were about 70 of them. So, with the vehicles repaired and the convoy almost ready to go, I called them all together.

'What we are going to do,' I announced, 'is line everything up on the main road and on Thursday morning, about an hour before dawn, we will leave.'

There had been a lot of rumours flying around – UNITA this and UNITA that, UNITA are still in the area . . . So I got the Filipinos together.

'All the workers know that we are going to leave at 4 a.m. on Thursday,' I told them. 'So the best thing we can do is surprise everybody.' (UNITA almost certainly had its informers among the Angolans.) 'We will leave on Wednesday morning, a day early.'

So that was what happened. Before first light on Wednesday the convoy rumbled out of Cafunfo. It included a lot of earth-moving equipment, graders, motor scrapers and so on, and FAPLA provided the escort. The only trouble was that FAPLA commandeered all the Intraco Land Rovers in Cafunfo – we had had a delivery of new Land Rovers before the February attack – and they commandeered our drivers and put them into uniform as well. Personally I did not go with the convoy. I got on the radio and said to my boss, 'O.k., the convoy has gone, but I will stay on here in Cafunfo just in case something happens.'

Something did happen. The morning after the convoy left I was standing outside the workshop with an English lad, George Patterson, who had come down from Dundo for Diamang. Suddenly there was a thump and we could feel the air move.

'What do you think that was?' said George, obviously nervous.

'Sounds like a landmine,' I said. 'Either close and a small one or a long way away and a big one.'

We radioed back to Dundo to tell them a landmine had gone off to the east, and MATS flew out one of their white security lads – ex-SAS, about sixteen of them in all. Unlike the DSD, though, they were not armed.

We did not need him to tell us what happened because within an hour of the landmine exploding they were bringing the bodies back. It was nothing to do with the convoy; it was a single truck, a Mazda 30-cwt, and it had hit an anti-tank mine about ten miles out of Cafunfo, on the crest of a hill, which is normal practice. I think that mine was meant for the convoy, but a day late. There were about three killed and eight injured.

The MATS people asked me: 'Don't you think it's dangerous?'

'I think we are safe enough in Cafunfo itself,' I said. 'Outside, o.k., it is dangerous.' At that, they flew straight back to Dundo, George Patterson and the rest of them, and I never saw them again.

My Intraco boss, Duncan Angus, called me up on the radio: 'Now that the convoy has gone,' he said, 'you had better come back.'

'Look,' I retorted, 'there is a lot of work to be done here and we can start now and get on with it.'

I was totally fed up with hanging around Andrada.

'Is it safe up there?' he asked.

'There's no problem in Cafunfo,' I said.

So in the end he told me to carry on and started sending me support. I was asking for mechanics, electricians, food and supplies to get Cafunfo working again. MATS' area manager for the whole of Angola, an Englishman named Brian Ainsley, came down by plane to see what Intraco was up to. But though I was English too and the only other white man there, he totally ignored me. He was highly tee'd off because Intraco was putting him under pressure to bring his crews back in, which he did not want to do.

Then news came of the convoy. I had not been worried, because the landmine did not prove that UNITA was still around; they could easily have set it up before they pulled out. But then the convoy – which was very slow, of course, with all that heavy machinery – was ambushed when it reached Quitapa bridge. UNITA blew up the bridge ahead of it, and when the convoy tried to turn round and go back, it found itself surrounded. About 22 FAPLA were killed in this shindig, and all our Land Rovers were blown up or shot to shreds. Only one got back, driven by a half-caste lad, Palestino, who worked for Intraco.

'How the hell did you get back?' I asked him, amazed.

'I don't know. I just took a chance. I have a few bullet holes in my Land Rover but nothing in vital places. I've come for food.' They had been completely stuck out there and had asked him to try to get through as they had no food or anything.

'There is no way you will get back,' I said to Palestino.

'Let me try,' he replied.

So he took food and he did get through. He was a brave lad. But the convoy was in a grim situation. One FAPLA lieutenant and eight soldiers changed into civvies and tried to get out, but they were wiped out. I was told UNITA strung their bodies upside down from trees, then cut the heads off and left the heads on the ground. At least that was the story.

In the end FAPLA brought up helicopter gunships from Luanda, and air-borne commandoes, using single-engine aircraft, P7s or P8s, a bit like Spitfires, to rescue the convoy. These went in and blasted UNITA. Then, with all the earth-moving equipment the convoy had, they bulldozed in the damaged bridge section and finally they got through to Andrada. I had had to send one of my crane-drivers as a driver for a Land Rover, and he got killed. They brought the body back. It arrived in Cafunfo at about 4 p.m., and his family surrounded my house. They were chanting, and they kept the chanting up till about 2 a.m. I kept my head down. Though it wasn't my fault, I thought it best to keep a low profile.

Gradually I started getting Cafunfo organized and building up a workforce. Two things I am good at are co-ordination and organization, and soon everyone knew that that nutcase Glen Dixon had taken over Cafunfo. The 'Portacabin' flew us in beds, pots and pans, and so forth, and Cookie, my old Filipino

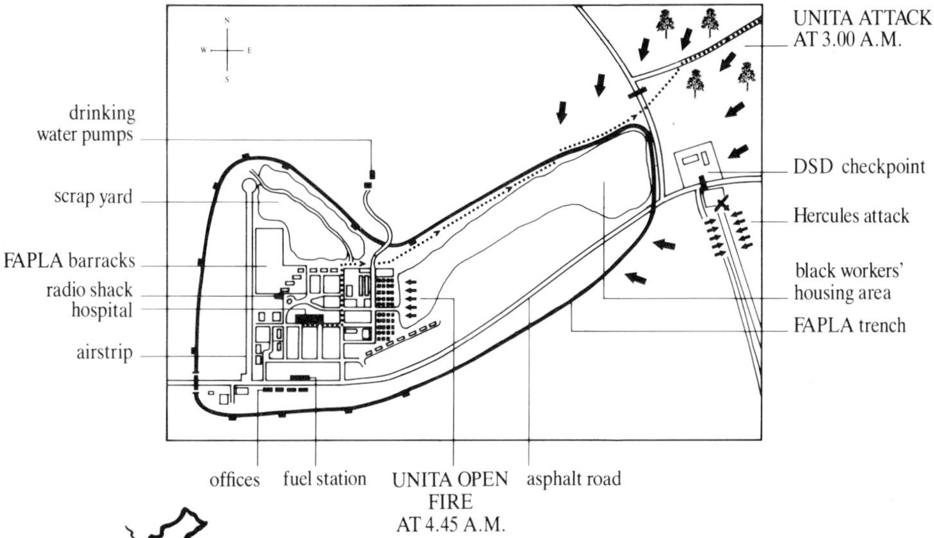

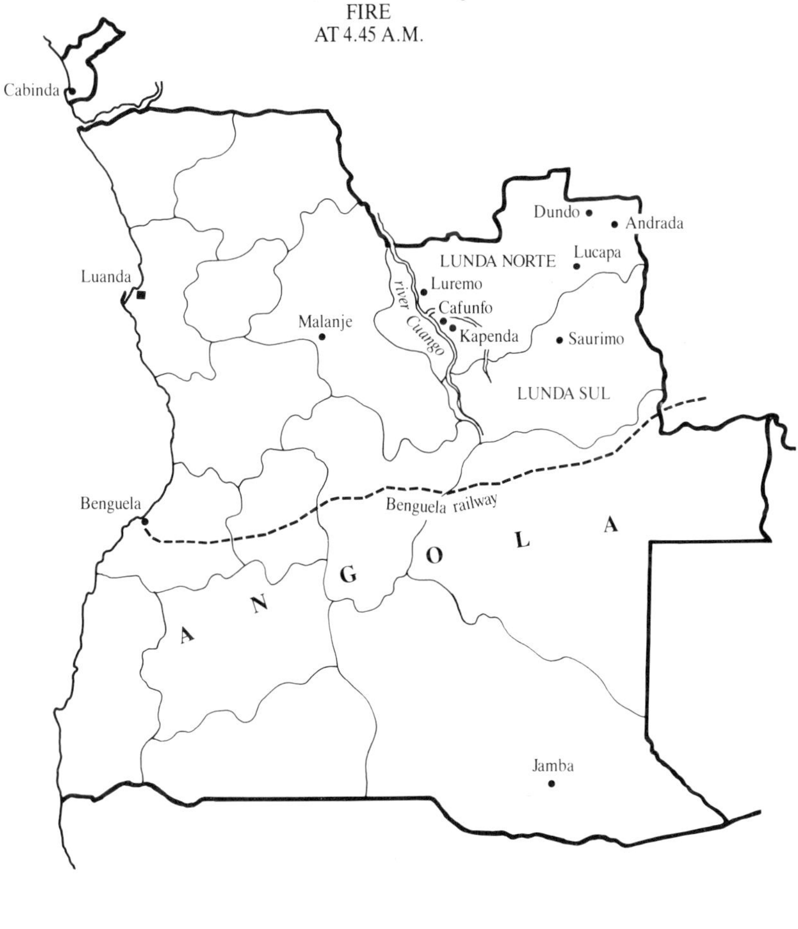

Top: diagram of the compound at Cafunfo, where the UNITA attack took place.

Bottom: province map of Angola.

The river-bed at Cafunfo, nearly ready for diamond extraction.

De-watering the diamond beds.

Diversion of the river Cuango for diamond-mining.

en Dixon's house
Cafunfo.

1
2
3
4
CAT
9
10
11
12
INTRACO
17
18
19

Glen Dixon (no. 13) with Intraco colleagues and crew:

no. 1, Obart;

2, Philip;

5, Jaspar (killed in Luanda);

6, Ephraim;

10, Tony Beer (who took Christmas leave);

12, Arthur Jones (also took Christmas leave);

14, Big Ted;

15, Cookie;

16, Roddy, the doctor;

17, Francis, the *abuelo*;

19, Angel;

21, another one who took Christmas leave.

Unloading stores from the cargo hold of a Hercules aircraft at Cafunfo. It was in just such a situation that co-pilot Bill Reed was killed during the UNITA attack.

Glen Dixon in the bachelor room at Lucapa.

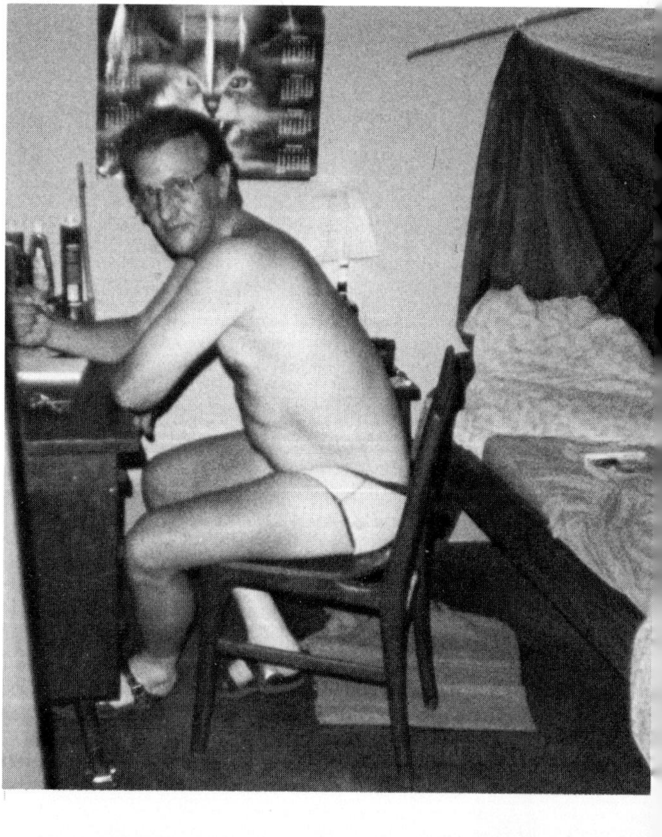

UNITA chief Dr Jonas Savimbi, for whom the hostages waited at Jamba. (*The Photo Source*)

Left to right: John MacMichael, Glen Dixon and Paul Huggins at the pres conference at Jamba, Angola, on the occasion of their release by UNITA on 1 March 1985. UNITA's flag can be seen on the wall behind them. (*Associate Press Photos*)

cook whom I had requested. I also requested two more British expatriates, Tony Beer and a lad called Arthur Jones. Arthur was a Welshman, a big lad. He walked like a ruptured duck but he was an excellent man for getting things done fast. One of his trades was that of electrician. The generating station had been totally destroyed at Cafunfo, and the transformers, carrying 6000 volts, shot out. But he got a generator in and another transformer, and then one evening when it was just getting dark, about three minutes past six, we were all sitting there on the verandah waiting for it, and lo and behold the street lights came on all over Cafunfo. All the Angolans were out on the town that night cheering and laughing: they had lived in total darkness for four months or so. The kids were playing in the streets till the early hours of the morning, thanks to Big Arthur.

Tony Beer had been at one of the outlying mines, a place called Mogis, about fifteen miles away, during the attack the previous February. He had lost radio contact with base, so he had just sat tight for a day and listened to UNITA banging away; then he loaded up his jeep and escaped to Luanda. He volunteered to come back down, so that made three Brits, and then they sent me some Intraco Portuguese, including a lad named Alberto who was a good mechanic but very nervous.

There was one man I particularly wanted who had worked with me in Lucapa. He was an Angolan, but he had been educated in Zaire and been to college in Zambia. His English was impeccable and he acted as a secretary and translator combined.

This guy was into everything. He was a real rogue, but a good lad. You had to let him go so far and just keep wiping his feet out from under him once a week, to keep him steady. But Jasper – that was his name – did not want to come down to Cafunfo at all. He wasn't a Marxist by any means; he was more for UNITA. But at the same time he was afraid of UNITA. That was why I wanted him there. My idea was that as he was afraid for his own skin, he was going to look after himself – and us too, indirectly. All I would have to do would be to keep an eye on him, and, whatever he did, act accordingly. So down he came, and he had a free hand as regards mixing with the people.

The Filipinos were nervous too, at first. Four or five were lads that I had asked to volunteer to come down with me from Lucapa, but the rest were recruited directly from the Philippines for Cafunfo and they had no idea what they were letting themselves in for. I did have some problems at first; some lads even locked themselves into their rooms and refused to work – you had to throw them in at the deep end. But Francis – he had come down from Cafunfo with me – could jolly them along. As explained earlier, he was their *abuelo*, or 'grandfather'. Filipinos like living together, all squashed up, and every group of Filipinos elects one. If they have any personal problems and they don't want to talk to the boss about it – one of the lads might have VD, or problems at home, or something he is afraid to talk to him about – then they will go to the 'grandfather'. The grandfather will deal with it as far as he is able, and if he cannot deal with it, then he will come to the boss. A lot depends on his character. I put Francis' name forward for *abuelo*, and they elected him. Many a time lads would come to me with a problem, but they would bring Francis with them.

There was only one lad who was entirely unsuitable and whom we had to send back. In general Filipinos are very adaptable to circumstances, very placid. Besides, they were on a nine months' hard-currency contract, with a month's paid leave at the end of it, and some were earning $1000 a week, paid in US dollars directly to the Philippines: this is four or five times the normal salary a Filipino would earn, even supposing he could find work at home.

The Filipinos got on with the Angolans better than anyone else – Portuguese, English or American. They picked up Portuguese very quickly because Spanish is one of their languages and Spanish and Portuguese are very close. Some of the Filipinos couldn't speak much English, though, only a sort of butchered version. But Francis had a very good command of American English and of Portuguese. That was one of the reasons all the other lads respected him.

Normally in Africa companies are not allowed to employ other Third World people. In most countries, like Nigeria and Ethiopia, they had their own good mechanics and electricians and so on. But Angola is a special case. Since the revolution there has been very little technical education – no training, nothing. There were old mechanics from the pre-revolutionary days, but they had not been able to keep up with modern technology. There just wasn't the knowledge. So it was agreed with Diamang that we, that's to say Intraco, could bring Filipinos in. Mechanically and electrically Filipinos are very good, better than a lot of British lads. And we needed them because Intraco has a massive operation in Angola. It has a Caterpillar fleet of about 460 vehicles in all: haul trucks, wheel-type loaders, truck-type loaders, motor scrapers, bull-dozers, compactors, loader-generators, wheel-type tractors, as well as at least 250 items of non-Caterpillar equipment.

Mr Hilinger, the man who interviewed me for the job in London, is vice-president of the whole company; the president and real boss is, I believe, a Greek, a multi-millionaire with headquarters in Lexington Avenue, New York; but Mr Hilinger runs the whole Angolan operation from Luanda. The Angola project is one of the biggest Caterpillar dealerships in the world, and, generally speaking, one of the biggest maintenance contracts of this type anywhere. Mr Hilinger has taken some extraordinary chances – like financing the purchase of all this Caterpillar equipment through an Intraco subsidiary – but when he takes chances, the gamble always seems to come off.

In the province of Lunda Norte there were about 200 expatriate workers in all, but only 17 English working for Intraco. The rest were Filipinos and Portuguese, mostly at the main workshops in Andrada. Intraco has been in Lunda Norte since 1977, since the decision was taken to bring in foreigners to run the mines for Angola.

In Cafunfo, each Filipino was more or less a master mechanic. The Angolans were split up into groups, so under each Filipino there would be a junior mechanic and two helpers – the electrical group, the welding group, the heavy track group and engine group, the transmission group and so on. We were a totally self-contained unit with our own electricians, mechanics, welders, power generators, advisers, specialists. We had our own cook, Cookie. The doctor-surgeon, Roddy, looked after our health but he also did lots of other jobs as well, supervising hygiene, camp activities and so forth.

One thing he had difficulty with was getting the lads to take their malaria tablets. It was only once a week, but to make the Filipinos take a malaria tablet Roddy had to stand there with their weekly issue of beer and cigarettes, put the tablet in their mouths on their tongues and make them swallow. Only once he had checked that the tablet was swallowed would he issue them with the beer and cigarettes, otherwise they just didn't get any. That is how serious it was. The Filipinos did not like the malaria tablet because they thought it made them go grey, it gave them diarrhoea, it made them infertile, it stopped them getting an erection . . . God knows how many complaints.

Once a week the Filipinos and myself would hold a weekly meeting. I had made them a recreation room, 26 by 12 feet, with a big television and video recorder, and a bar, and it was all done out in Filipino style. That is where I would hold the weekly pow-wow. All I had to say could usually be said in five minutes, but we would blather on, and sometimes I would be there for three hours, just talking and answering questions. One of the troubles was that the Filipinos had a lot of time on their hands. We were on an 8-hour day, working a 48-hour week, and at Saturday lunchtime we were finished. In working hours we could go out 25 or 30 miles but in leisure no more than 7 kilometres (4 miles) – MATS orders – and the river was 4½ miles away. So there was no fishing or swimming. One of the greatest problems for all of us was killing time.

We tried to organize table tennis, badminton, barbecues – that sort of thing. This was part of Roddy's job and he was pretty good at it. Then we were getting about 10 videos a week, but we got bored with them. Employees could not drink because they only had one case of beer a week – a case of beer or a bottle of whisky, plus a case of soft drinks and a carton of cigarettes. On the black market a carton of 200 Benson & Hedges cigarettes was worth about 15,000 *kwanza*; the salary for a top Angolan mechanic working for Diamang was 10,000 *kwanza* a month: in other words it would take him six weeks' work to earn just 200 cigarettes, without anything else.

So two things started to happen: gambling and women. One Filipino, called Angel, was a grandfather nine times over. Celibacy was not natural for them, and, as far as women were concerned, the only thing to do was to turn a blind eye as long as the top Angolan management wives did not become involved. When we arrived there were already three small Filipino-black half-castes wandering around Cafunfo, so the previous Filipinos had been proving their worth over that time.

The gambling was a different kettle of fish; that had to be stopped. The Filipinos had cheque books with them, so they were even writing out cheques and gambling away not only their black-market money but the dollars that were being paid to them back in the Philippines. It got to the stage where I had to ban cigarettes and drink to stop the gambling. If I caught two or three men gambling, I would say: 'No cigarettes or beer for a month.' That slowed it down, though it still went on. I had to act as a sort of disciplinarian because, though the Filipinos are hard workers and very easy to get on with, they are very innocent, unsophisticated, placid people, very trusting, and I was responsible for them.

Lynn came out to join me for a three-month visit on 7 September. I organized a bungalow and had it re-painted and fitted out with new furniture, which my boss sent up on a Hercules.

On the morning of the 9th, UNITA hit Luremo mine, about 15 miles north-west of us. The whole town was out watching the smoke from the burning machines. We lost five machines, and some of our workers were captured and killed. That afternoon Peter Heap, the MATS area mining manager, a man whom I liked and had worked under at Lucapa, flew down from Dundo.

'I have come to look at Luremo,' he said. 'I flew over it, and it looks like we have lost some plant. I have a spare seat in the plane. I advise you to let me take your wife out.' (She was the only white woman in Cafunfo, I should explain.)

'No, I can't do that,' I said.

'Why not?'

'I have my reasons, and besides, we are safe at the moment.'

I had reason to think we were pretty secure. We had had about five months of peace from UNITA at this time. It was the dry season, when there are no leaves on the trees to provide cover for forces approaching from afar, and Jasper, the Angolan secretary/translator, seemed to think there was no imminent danger. He was not worried about the Luremo situation: 'It's only a small group;' he told me: 'We're o.k.' Jasper had special instructions to tell me straight away if anything serious was in the offing and then I would have flown Lynn out to Andrada. I was relying on Jasper to look after Lynn's skin as well as his own. What was more, if Lynn had left, the Filipinos would have wanted to go.

However, Peter left ten minutes after our conversation, and I wondered if I had made the right decision.

To deal with the Luremo raiders eight helicopters, small French Alouettes, were flown in, and two big Russian helicopter gunships. They would be going out and coming back every three-quarters of an hour; a 12-ton truck, loaded with ammunition, was also sent. Within two days the two big gunships alone had used all that ammunition up. They were similar to the helicopter gunships the Americans used in Vietnam, rocket pods and all. I watched one of them hovering about 10 feet off the ground at the end of the runway, firing off its cannon and whole magazines – God knows what at. After it had gone the runway was just littered with shells. They had Cuban pilots: maybe this one was just trigger-happy. You could pick out the Cuban pilots because they wore tan belts and tan holsters with pistols while everyone else in uniform had deep red mahogany-coloured leather belts.

There were a couple of Russians with them: one was a pilot, a big lad, the other a small guy. They came in their own aircraft. They had trouble with a Renault diesel generator starter motor, so they came to us. There was this big black guy with them who spoke Russian and Portuguese and I had Jasper with me, who spoke Portuguese and English, so the translation was a bit stretched. We were chatting away and tried to help them but didn't succeed. We invited them for a drink that night, but they did not come.

We invited the Cuban pilots for a drink too, but the Cubans were not allowed to come to our house. They were very definitely military. They would not talk to the Filipinos, though they were all Spanish-speaking. They did not even socialize with the Angolans. The Russians did not socialize with the Cubans and, though the Angolan troops who had come in were good troops, commandoes, and the Cubans were their allies, the Cubans did not socialize with them. There was a very distinct barrier there between these so-called allies.

About 300 FAPLA commandoes also came in. They were very different from the garrison troops. The garrison consisted just of local lads: someone had put a rifle in their hands and taught them to point it in the right direction and that was about it. They seemed such a slap-happy outfit. I never saw anyone saluting, for instance. But these FAPLA commandoes saluted, and when they marched they all marched spot-on. The FAPLA garrison troops had had no drill or proper training. (On the other hand, I have to say that they were better disciplined than the garrisons elsewhere in Lunda Norte. In Lucapa or Andrada or Dundo they were really wild; every night there would be shooting, sometimes single shots, sometimes whole magazines let off, usually at shadows: there was no discipline or fire-control at all. But I knew one FAPLA lad in Cafunfo who shot himself through the foot, and he was put in jail for three months for making a noise in the night. We only heard shooting sporadically, about three times in six or seven months. So our FAPLA garrison was nowhere near as bad as the other FAPLA troops in the province.)

Soon the commandoes, helicopters and gunships were gone – everything gone. The only thing left was a P8, a Spitfire-type plane, that had touched down, had a blow-out, veered off the runway and gone into the bush on its nose. There was that – and its Cuban pilot. He had to stay behind and guard it as he was the one who had cracked it up. So he was the only Cuban we had in Cafunfo and he was there for weeks. We sent messages inviting him for a drink but he never came. If he had still been there during the attack, UNITA would have killed him.

A week after the raid on Luremo FAPLA caught three Angolan guys – UNITA, they said. Two were handcuffed and taken off to Dundo, but one 'died of injuries' in jail, whatever that meant. About a fortnight after that, at the beginning of October, Jasper took me aside.

'UNITA is in the bush,' he said.

'How close?'

'About 14 or 15 kilometres' (8½–9 miles).

'What size group?'

'I don't know,' he said, 'but UNITA is there in the bush. I want to leave.' He was getting really nervous. From what I could tell later this would have been about the time UNITA was beginning to infiltrate its troops north, not just the local group.

'No, no,' I said to Jasper, 'slow down.'

We did have a landmine or two that we reckoned the Luremo raiders had left behind. Our low-loader set one off when it was carrying a large drag line outside Cafunfo. Arthur, the big Welshman, drove up about a minute later, looked at this smoking hole and the low-loader and started cursing. He had been struggling to get this machine in for three weeks and had thought he was on the last lap. And there it was, all the bodywork blown to shreds. But he was lucky, really. He had been driving up and down that particular road for three weeks in his jeep. UNITA had probably buried the landmine 10–12 inches below the surface, so it needed 60 or 70 pounds of pressure per square inch to set it off. However, had it been just below the surface, needing only 2–3 lbs pressure, that would have been it for Arthur in his jeep.

Despite Jasper's fears, all remained quiet in the weeks that followed. Lynn had stayed on as arranged after the Luremo raid; all the time she was there, the Filipinos were quite happy about security. If I had sent her away earlier than arranged, there would have been a panic, but on 6 December she was due to go back to the UK in the normal way. She had been out three months, so she left, and Tony Beer went with her, for his Christmas leave. He had a pet monkey called Fred, about three or four months old, and I promised to look after Fred for him. That was one promise, as it turned out, I could not keep.

Arthur and six Filipinos went on leave too, on 17 December, and the very next day UNITA struck again. This time they hit Luzamba. Luzamba was quite a sizeable place, a mining town of about 40 houses; but it was nearly two hours' drive outside Cafunfo, the last outlying mine to the south, in the opposite direction from Luremo. As it was so far away we had not started up production. It was maintained, that was all. There was no machinery there, only generators, because we had cleared it all out, so there was not really much for UNITA to destroy.

But the Angolans had known something was in the air. For about three weeks before the attack on 18 December they had been sleeping out in the bush. Some of the mechanics would come in all bleary-eyed in the morning.

'Bloody hell,' I would say, 'you'll have to stop getting your leg over!'

'I've been sleeping in the bush, boss.'

'What did you sleep in the bush for?'

'Maybe UNITA come.'

It was always maybe this, maybe that. But all these things were building up and by this time Jasper was a bag of nerves. Among the Angolans at Cafunfo there were two groups, one pro the government and one pro UNITA, and Jasper was caught between them – piggy-in-the-middle. After the attack on Luzamba he was really jittery. He wanted to go home for Christmas at least, and on 21 December I gave him permission and he got a flight out to Luanda. But without Jasper my sources of information dried up. I could feel something was wrong, but I couldn't put a finger on it. It was a kind of fear among the Angolans, particularly in the workshop. They all wanted to leave Cafunfo. The foreman in the workshop was demanding to go home and see his folks at Christmas.

'You've only just come back off leave,' I said. 'You haven't been back a month and you're due to stay six months before you go back home.'

'I have to go,' he said. 'It is urgent.'

In the end I agreed, and off he went. But I refused to sign the other lads' tickets, and that was the only way they could get out of Cafunfo. They had to stay. I would find them standing around in little groups talking and I'd ask what the problem was, trying to find out if this was just the pre-Christmas attitude. But it was more than that, though I couldn't nail it down. They kept looking here and there. There were lots of squabbles and arguments, and fights in the workshop. There was a strange feeling everywhere.

Even we few remaining Britons were getting up each other's noses. The MATS area manager at Cafunfo, Jim Taggart, was a Geordie (both my parents were Geordies) and a nice bloke, but stubborn in some things.

'When are you going out to Luzamba?' I asked him.

'I'm waiting for an escort, and so on,' he said.

'If it's possible, I'd like to go with you.'

'Yes, o.k.'

A new Briton had arrived the day before – this was John, John MacMichael – and unbeknownst to me he and Jim plus an escort went off to Luzamba to inspect the damage. I was mad as a wet hen about this.

'Well,' I said when they came back, 'what's the crack?'

'It was nothing to do with you,' said Jim Taggart. 'There was no Intraco equipment out there.'

'I don't agree with you,' I said. 'It's to do with all of us. I want to go out and see the damage and estimate how big the force was that hit it.'

So he started trying to describe how Luzamba looked. But I cut him off.

'To see it for oneself, that's a totally different thing from hearing it described,' I said.

I was missing Jasper more and more. But there was nothing definite, just something there that did not tally. I thought to myself, we'll get New Year over and then I will start reducing the crew. But at the time there seemed no reason to evacuate. There were no reports coming in. I would go round to the chief of the DSD, Selgado, and say: 'Why are people so edgy? Is UNITA closing in, or what?'

'No, absolutely no problem,' he would reply. 'If UNITA ever do attack, you will be the first one to know. We will escort you out of Cafunfo with all your crew.'

Then, two days before Christmas, Selgado himself left for Dundo – almost all the DSD lads, incidentally, about 200 of them, were out at the various mines, not in Cafunfo itself. The town was defended by our FAPLA garrison and by this new trench system they had dug all around the town, with an open field of fire cleared in front of it. That was new since the February attack; manned night and day, it was a bit like a mediaeval wall surrounding and protecting a city, at least in concept.

For the Filipinos Christmas Eve is the big celebration, so we gave a party in our bar. Some of the lads put together this big Christmas tree and the electrician had it sparkling, as well as stars shining all over the compound and lights flashing 'Merry Christmas'. So it was a different atmosphere. The tape recorder was playing 'White Christmas', which was a little strange, really, because the weather was nice and warm – not hot, but very pleasant. We had been sent lots of goodies by our bosses including two pigs from Germany. One was barbecued in the Filipino fashion, one roasted in the English fashion. We invited all the British lads – Jim Taggart, Peter Hewitt and John MacMichael – and the Portuguese working for MATS, five or six of them, and we had a damn good night. The beer was free, and Roddy the doctor, who was in charge of the entertainment, organized the singing. The Filipinos had some very good singers and they sang a lot of the old 'fifties and 'sixties favourites. Then the Portuguese came in, with their sentimental Portuguese *fados*. It was two in the morning before everyone went away, legless.

On Christmas Day all the British were invited to a Christmas dinner, and then in the afternoon we sat there drinking wine and watching videos and having a good time. The Filipinos did not have a priest but Roddy organized some sort of service for them. The project manager in Andrada had asked me to send him Roddy temporarily over the Christmas period as Intraco had over 100 Filipinos at Andrada and their doctor-surgeon had gone on leave. Under normal circumstances I would have sent him but all my Filipinos were very jittery and Roddy had a stabilizing effect on them. 'Not possible,' I radioed back, 'urgently needed here.' As it turned out, though I could hardly have foreseen it at the time, this was one of the best decisions I made, to keep Roddy behind with us at Cafunfo.

On Boxing Day we just lounged about and then on the 27th, the Thursday, we went back to work, but not at a hard pace. There was too much in the atmosphere to push too hard. We felt that if we pushed too hard there would be an explosion, and we would be in the middle of it. So we just went along gently. I sent one Filipino needing dental treatment and another, who had passport problems, by plane to Dundo, and told them both to stay there until I gave permission for them to come back: two down, seventeen to go.

New Year's Eve was going to be the following Monday, and New Year's Day Tuesday, so the plan was to work all Saturday, then take the three days off. The big Diamang boss, Dr Makenda, came up in a helicopter with a load of ministers on Friday. He, they and Jim Taggart flew off to inspect Luzamba, returning that afternoon. Then the bigwigs went off. Jim Taggart called me over to his office.

'I want you to go to Luzamba and repair the generators that have been blown up,' he said.

'No way,' I replied. 'If I'm not allowed to go with you when you are escorted, I'm buggered if I am going on my own.'

'I just want you to go there and look at the damage,' he said, trying to calm me down.

'No,' I said, 'I am quite within my rights if I refuse to go to Luzamba. I will not go and I will not send anyone else. I am not being difficult but I am not going to Luzamba on my own.'

'O.k.,' he said. 'Will you go with me and with a DSD escort?'

'Yes, o.k.,' I replied.

So we arranged it for the next day, the morning of Saturday 29 December. The DSD agreed to meet us near the runway at the barrier by their barracks at 8 a.m. That was one rendezvous we never kept. I went across on Friday evening to have a chat with the Filipinos, came back, read a book, and about ten o'clock I went to bed, lights out.

It had just been a normal working day. What was not normal – though I didn't know it at the time – was that within an hour, by eleven o'clock, all the Angolans had left the town, all 2,500 of them: workers, management, families, virtually every single person. They just vanished into the bush. You can't blame them, but the disconcerting thing about it was that they all knew without a shadow of a doubt that UNITA was coming that night.

In England two days later, on that New Year's Eve that was never to be celebrated in Cafunfo, the BBC's six o'clock news carried a report from its Washington correspondent that in Angola, Africa, UNITA had raided a mining town in the north-east and had taken prisoners, among them two Americans and three British citizens – Mr John MacMichael, Mr Paul Huggins and Mr Glen Dixon. One hour earlier, at Burton-on-the-Wolds, Lynn had been telephoned by Intraco's London office, who warned her that this would be on the news but reassured her that I was alive and, as far as they knew, o.k.

By then, of course, we had been marching for two days.

Chapter IV

The Long March: 1

I think the saddest sight I saw in those first two days was Fred, strapped to the front bumper of a Land Rover with a piece of cord around his stomach. He was squealing and looking terrified, and he was on my conscience because I had not kept my promise to Tony Beer that I would look after him properly. For these UNITA lads, Fred was a meal. That was a shame because, for a monkey, he had been a nice character.

Every vehicle that could run in Cafunfo had been taken by UNITA and loaded up. They had emptied the stores, everything. I would say that, booty apart (and there was plenty of that, from clothes and blankets to radios and television sets which needed two men to carry them), they must have brought something like 60 or 70 tons of food out of Cafunfo – including half a ton of Beck's beer. The UNITA soldiers carried everything: their own food, their own cooking utensils, their own ammunition, and so on. They came out well loaded and they were staggering for the first week. How they marched I don't know. We were just carrying ourselves, and we were really struggling. These guys were carrying something like 45 to 50 lbs – probably 60 in some cases.

I remember one night I bumped into the back of one lad who had a sack on his head. It was full of tins of sardines. This sack fell between us, landed on my feet and creased them up. I tried to help him to pick this thing up and it took me all my strength to lift it chest high, so that he could get underneath to get it on his head again. He was carrying also a pack and four or five bandoliers (they are about 3-4 lbs each), plus pouches on the side of his belt full of ammunition. He also had his raincoat and his cape and his rifle. Some were carrying landmines on their heads, some were carrying bazookas – it was unreal, what they were carrying.

For the first three or four days we were following an old track, so the Land Rovers were continually running to and fro past us. This meant that, to start with, we had good food: rice, tuna fish, corned beef, things like that – in small quantities, admittedly, but nourishing. For instance, the evening after we were captured, we had a tin of tuna and a can of beer each and I managed to get a Schweppes tonic water. Then I had an idea.

'Hang on to the beer cans,' I said to the lads. 'They'll be useful for carrying water.'

As for me, I never let the tonic bottle out of my pocket. The beer was the first and last we were to see until Jamba, and everyone except the Portuguese arrived there still carrying their cans.

Meanwhile the UNITA lads all around were lighting their fires and cooking their dinners. We wondered at the time how they dared light fires when we were only six or seven miles from Cafunfo.

'The airforce always go home at 5 p.m.,' they explained. 'Always. They never fly after 5 p.m. Also, we have killed most of FAPLA, so who is going to give us any trouble?'

They were certainly proud of having captured Cafunfo again. They might have looked like a rag-tag mob, a bunch of hooligans – and no wonder, because some of them had been several months in the bush and everything they wore was clapped out – but they were well organized. They had 2-inch mortar platoons, 4-inch mortar platoons, light machine-gun and heavy machine-gun platoons, catering platoons, medical platoons, plus sniper and marksman units. Later we were told that UNITA had seven battalions up in the north, with three more on the way, but that was probably an exaggeration. My estimate is that they had five battalions there, with maybe another two coming.

Each battalion consisted of 300 men, and certainly the attack on Cafunfo had been carried out by a brigade – that's to say it had been a three-battalion action. That first night the whole brigade, something like 1000 UNITA troops, was camped all around us. Most of the troops had radios, and they all tuned in to Radio Jamba to listen to their president, Jonas Savimbi. Every night, at 7 p.m. precisely, he would come on the air to talk to his troops in the field, and feed them information back about successful attacks or anything else that might have come up. It was an unvarying ritual, and if Savimbi was not available himself for any reason, his second-in-command would speak in his place. These broadcasts were beamed over 600 miles, as the crow flies, almost from one end of Angola to the other, so Radio Jamba's transmitters must have been extremely powerful.

Then all the fires were put out, all the radios turned off, and there was total silence throughout the night; you could have heard a pin drop.

That first night was very dark; there was no moon and it was overcast and cloudy. It was still the rainy season in Angola, and though the weather had been nice and warm over Christmas, it was to be wet, wet and wet again during the next few weeks. The humidity was dense; there were to be torrential rainstorms, drizzle, the lot – very demoralizing; yet in a way it was a lifesaver for us. I doubt any of us would have survived the march if it had been the hot season. Seven-tenths of the time it was overcast, and the remaining three-tenths of the time it was raining.

That first night it started to drizzle at about 10 p.m. The Filipinos had grabbed most of the blankets, laid them out four in a row on the ground, then piled themselves together on top and covered themselves with four more. But we whites, we were not well acquainted enough to huddle together. We were all standoffish. It was a miserable night. I didn't sleep at all. It was too cold, too damp; and also I was too wound up. I suspect we all were – worrying about what the future was to hold.

Not that the night lasted all that long. They woke us at 4 a.m., in the dark (this was to be the usual ritual), gave us each an inch-square cube of ham from a tin for breakfast, and then we were up on our feet and on our way, stumbling and banging about till the grey dawn appeared.

Cafunfo is high in the hills, and the country over which we were walking was hilly and wooded, with lots of streams. We would cross something like a stream an hour, on average. The trouble was that a lot of these streams flowed into open valleys, covered with swamp grass 18 inches high. Underfoot we would be walking on swamp, black silty stuff. There we had to be careful to walk flat on our feet. If you tried to walk on your toes, you just sank right down up to your crutch, and it was only your crutch that kept you from sinking in any further. It was really painful for some of us – particularly for me, as my heels were in tatters very soon and having to put my weight on them was pure agony. The swamps would eventually peter out into murky water, which we would have to wade across.

But this was basically uphill and downdale work. It was too much for Hobart early on. The oldest of the Filipinos, he had problems breathing – a bad chest. He collapsed about half-way up one hill. He was that shattered, he couldn't get up. One of the UNITA escort literally jerked him up off the ground by his ear. As luck would have it, Roddy saw this happen and reported it to me, and I reported it to the English-speaking lieutenant colonel. I ought to say that that was the worst incident that happened on the trail. There was no brutality: just a certain amount of shoving and forcible encouragement to keep moving. In this particular case the soldier was reprimanded at once.

The other hostage who simply could not keep up, because he had smashed up the sides of his feet jumping out of the Hercules, was the Captain. Two of us were walking, one on either side of him, helping him along, and he was trying to move on the balls of his feet only. By 10 o'clock, after six hours' marching, when we halted, he just could not walk any further. In the end we asked the lieutenant colonel if it would be possible to put both him and Hobart on a Land Rover, and this was agreed. We didn't see them very much after that. They were in the cabin of a Land Rover. That saved them a lot of aggro.

We had stopped in a very sparse spinney, and UNITA started cutting trees down. We couldn't fathom this. What they were making was three forks. They set these forks up – a straight piece of trunk between two forks standing in the ground, with another trunk across this way and a trunk across that way, making it like a square. We asked: 'What is it for?'

'For you to sit and eat on it,' they said.

So the idea was that you'd park your backside on it – it was about a foot off the ground – and put your meal on your knees.

'We are going to get fed?' I asked.

'Yes,' they said. And they brought us rice, and tinned fish – anchovies in tomato sauce – and that was good.

But by this time we all had blisters on our feet. I had four blisters and this UNITA medic came up, got hold of these blisters with some tweezers, pulled them up and then cut and broke them open. He filled them full with some red dye stuff, an antiseptic; I spotted the label, and it was from South Africa. It was miraculous. There was no great pain, and after six hours' rest I felt as sound as a bell.

I say 'rest', but once again it was miserable – this time because of tree ants. We were lying around under the trees, and down they came, big red ants, crawling all over us and biting like the clappers. At four o'clock in the afternoon – that's to say, only an hour and a half before night was due to fall – we were up and off again, down the track.

We had hardly been going half an hour when the lieutenant colonel's Land Rover overtook us, and pulled in. The lieutenant colonel got out, carrying a bundle wrapped in a rag. What he had inside that bundle for us was a real surprise: all our watches, whites' and Filipinos' alike, that had been stolen from us by UNITA shortly after we were captured. You have to give UNITA their due: they were pretty well disciplined, and they did their best to make up smartly for any mistakes that they might have made. I doubt whether in the British Army, in a similar situation where prisoners' watches had been looted, they would have been restored so quickly – or at all. The Filipinos were overjoyed. They really treasured those gold watches of theirs, and they perked up considerably now that they knew they were not going to be ill-treated, still less massacred, or even robbed. It was Roddy the doctor-surgeon who gave them confidence in their marching ability and kept up their mental state.

The lieutenant colonel was in fact commanding the battalion that was escorting us. As I said, he spoke very reasonable English and he took the trouble to explain to us what was going on.

'We are in a difficult position here,' he said, 'because we are not in UNITA country. This is FAPLA territory, and we will have to move quickly, and often by night. If FAPLA planes catch us out in the open, they will machine-gun and strafe our columns – and don't think they will show any restraint just because a handful of prisoners – yourselves – may be killed too. They won't. So we have three or four days' really fast and hard walking ahead of us. We have to cover a lot of distance. Then, after that, we can start taking it more easy.'

What confused me at the time was that we were obviously heading north-east, not south. It was quite easy to keep a sense of direction because we had the stars at night and the sun, occasionally, by day. I am a person who likes to know where he is as regards north, south, east and west. If I go to a strange hotel and I don't know where I am direction-wise, I will have a very disturbed night's sleep. (For some reason I always seem to sleep better when I face west.) So I made it my business to keep track of our direction during the march. For the first few days we continued to head east. In fact we headed north-east for about a week, swung round east-south-east for about another ten days, and then went south-west again till we hit the first major landmark that I was able to recognize: the Luanda-Saurimo asphalted road. We had come round in a vast letter C. Much later we were told that this was because FAPLA knew the route that the last group of hostages, from the February attack, had been marched down – a direct A-to-B shorter route – so this time it was essential to follow a much more indirect way round. This made sense in retrospect. But at the time it totally baffled us, as we seemed to be heading for the first week directly away from Jamba, towards the border with Zaire.

That second evening we had our first taste of a night march. It was only a short night march, because we stopped to camp at 10 p.m., but it was enough to make us dread them in future.

When it was a moonless night, it was as black as your hat, the sort of blackness that you would never get in England. You might be standing in the middle of Bradgate Park and you would always be able to see a faint glow from the lights of Leicester miles away. But in Angola it was black, black, black. The extraordinary thing was that UNITA appeared able to see in the dark, though *we* could not even make out the man three feet in front of us. We just stumbled along behind each other, and many times we would wander off the track, crashing into trees and branches, and they would have to come and drag us back into line again. Sometimes we would hold on to the straps of the pack of the man in front of us, like blind men clinging on to guide-dogs. Other times we would ask them to put something light on their back, like a yellow cape that we could vaguely make out and follow.

But it was only too easy to start hallucinating: one moment we might think the man in front was still there; but in fact he was not, he had gone on. Paul and John suffered far worse from this than I did. They would find themselves walking away, imagining they were still with the group, without realizing what they were doing. And if we dropped out for a tinkle or whatever, we would suddenly lose all sense of direction and begin to panic. It was amazing that nobody – bar Bushbunny, and then, unfortunately, only for two days – became totally lost.

It rained again that night, but this time our escorts did what they could for us. They came round with spade-like implements – simple handles attached to blades – when we had halted; and dug a shallow trench, about six inches deep and nine inches wide, all around our sleeping site. The earth dug out was piled up in the middle. Then they flattened that, fixed two upright sticks in it, and raised a tarpaulin, what they called a *tarb*, about six foot square, over us. It had two brass holes in the middle, and one at each corner. Then they would weave grass into both ends, so that if the rain came down it would hit the grass and drip on to the floor rather than into the tent. The result was that whenever it rained it would fill the trench rather than the centre; and also we had soft material to lie on, earth piled up and then flattened out, free from ants and termites and so on. They would usually do this when we stopped for the night or when a storm was coming on. They would also build us a fire. We liked a fire right outside our tent, and as time wore on they knew that we liked the fire placed between our two tents, the Americans' tent and ours. So, whereas the Filipinos liked little individual fires, for us they would build one big log fire.

As time wore on too, we learnt how to build our own grass shelter for the three of us in twenty minutes flat. It would not have worked with English grass. What is needed is African grass, long and thin, the finer the better. The system, basically, is to start at the bottom, with clumps or fistfuls of grass about two feet high tied together with bark. We learnt a lot of things from UNITA and among them was how to choose and use bark. One particular type of tree was suitable. You make an incision at the bottom of the trunk about an inch wide, then get hold of a handful of the bark and just pull it, and it runs right up the tree. Then you remove the outer layer of soft white bark and you are left with this strip, about $1/16$–inch thick, that is extraordinarily strong and malleable. We used it to make carrying straps for our blankets, or to tie our shoes round our feet, as well as to string together these clumps of grass for the grass shelters. There the system was to build a framework, sticks tied together with bark; and then, beginnning at ground level, to spread out these long strings of bark attached to clumps of grass. Then you do the next level, just like laying tiles. When you approach the peak or crest, what you do is turn the grass the opposite way round and tie it in clumps about six inches apart, and the rain runs off as it would from a thatched roof; and so you stay dry.

We also soon learnt, from copying UNITA, how to get a good fire going quickly and how to keep it blazing. There is a particular plant, quite a common one, fortunately, that withers away in the dry season, leaving a long thin stick about ¼ inch in diameter, tapering off to zero. The system is to break a bunch of these up, throw a handful on the floor and build your fire on top. Within three or four minutes you have a blazing fire throwing out a lot of heat; and, even better, it burns slowly and will stay alight despite gusts of wind or drizzle or whatever. Many a time we would go out and collect this type of wood for ourselves, if our feet weren't feeling too bad.

Not that it was perfectly organized, that second night. We were cold and wet and depressed long before the shelters were up. But we had blankets and by now we were beginning to learn how to keep warm. We pulled the blanket up to just below our noses, and we would then breathe in through our noses and out through our mouths. That way cold air came in through our noses, and warm air went out of our mouths and circulated under the blanket.

The other trick was to wrap the blanket as loosely as possible around our bodies. If we wrapped ourselves tight, as we did instinctively at first, the body heat was transmitted straight through our skin into the blanket and out: wasted, instead of being conserved.

But the main thing, of course, was that we were losing our initial standoffishness and, to keep warm, we were beginning to huddle up together under the blankets, the two Americans in their tent and me and John in ours. Paul wouldn't sleep with us till much later. He had a very thick nylon blanket, about an inch thick; he would roll up in this blanket, and he was never cold. But John and I had two normal blankets and a very thin extra blanket that John had managed to fiddle from the transport. We would lay this thin blanket on the ground, then we would lay our shorts or trousers under where our bodies would be, use our shoes for a pillow, then lie down and pull our two blankets over us. It wasn't ideal. My blanket had two cuts in it, and every night I could feel the cold air coming in through these cuts. But there was no way you could sleep on your own. The Filipinos slept three or four together; and by cuddling up to each other John and I managed to sleep o.k.

Of all of us Al had the worst time. The Captain had managed, by creeping his way with UNITA, to get two blankets to Al's one. But instead of share and share alike, as John and I were doing, he insisted on keeping both for himself – one to lie on and one as a cover; whereas Al could only use his one as a cover and had to lie in the muck. Also, the Captain insisted in sleeping near the open end of the tarpaulin; and if Al went out and stepped on his blanket – even though he would be careful to be wearing socks only, not shoes, what a rumpus there would be. But Al never quarrelled. He would simply say, 'Sorry, mate.' He had the hardest time of all of us on the march – both because of the Captain and because of his own weak physical condition. But it did not seem to bother him at all. He never really got perturbed about anything. He could make a joke out of a serious situation. He was extremely easy-going, and he was a good morale-booster.

Sometimes we really needed our morale boosted. We would be split up or they wouldn't make a camp; they might just say, for instance, 'Rest for two hours.' Then we would just roll up in our blankets and crash out on the ground. We were so tired, cold and wet that we would just go to sleep. We probably slept half an hour to three-quarters of an hour before the cold got through to us. Then we would get up, shivering, and try to move around and get warm again. But on many occasions, particularly when it was raining, it was nearly impossible to recover the lost heat. Our blankets would be wet through, our teeth would be chattering, we would be suffering from cramp: but the amazing thing was that, for all that, not one of us went down with pneumonia or even a cold – and normally I am susceptible to colds. There must have been something that we were eating, or doing, that kept us healthy, at least in that way.

By the third day we were beginning to get into the swing of things. As usual we were woken up before dawn, and then there would be about an hour of packing up and shuffling and shunting, stopping and starting, before the column set out properly on the day's march. We, the hostages, were in the middle of the column, with our escort: and the whole column – the battalion of 300 (half in front of us, and half behind) – would stretch out like a school kids' crocodile for anything up to 2½ or 3 miles.

The scouting parties would probably be about two hours

ahead of us. That was one of the reasons why we saw so little wildlife on the march; by the time we were where the head of the column had been any animals had long since disappeared. Snakes, ground insects, scorpions and spiders, there were plenty of them – and beautiful birds too. But only once did we see a bushbuck. It had ducked down in the grass and tried to hide. But as we were marching past its nerve must have broken, and it ran. There was a group of young boys with the column, aged about 9 or 10; they weren't in uniform but they carried shotguns and sporting rifles. They were meant to be hunters, killing animals for food. There were about six or seven of them. They would drift away, sometimes for a couple of days at a time; but, as far as we could tell, they never succeeded in killing any game whatsoever – not once.

The first hour of the day's march was always mortal agony for me. Once the pace was set, off we would go, knowing that we would have to keep that pace up for six hours – six hours minimum. Somehow all the pain would seem to be coming from my feet. As we went on, the pain would even out between the feet; it was impossible to tell which was the more painful. Gradually the pain seemed to come up to the knees; it was just like a red glow below the knees. Then, once this had happened and the feet had warmed up, I knew that I could keep going.

We would even enjoy the dawns, and the scenery, once our muscles had warmed up. But for the first week the muscles in the backs of our necks ached like hell because our heads were always bent forward: 99 per cent of the time we were walking we couldn't lift our eyes up off the heels of the bloke in front – it was really depressing, a quick look up at the scenery, then down again – because we were on the look-out for lumps in the ground, our feet were so tender. But after the first hour, when the pain had dispersed and was all over instead of being concentrated in individual points, it wasn't so bad. We would probably go on like that for two or three hours. Then the pain would start again, and for the remaining couple of hours it would be a real effort to put one foot in front of the other. It would feel as if there were two raw lumps of meat on the ends of our legs.

Another major problem in those first few days was, rather surprisingly and despite the rain and the wet, thirst. We had always been very careful with the water at Cafunfo. There were three natural springs there, which had been capped and piped up into the town. So the water was pretty clean. Even so in the canteen my orders to everyone, Europeans and Filipinos alike, had been to drink only boiled and filtered water. We boiled it up in milk churns and then filtered it. We were always meticulous about that.

The very first day of the march, when we were almost dying of thirst, I had noticed in the bush a weed-like plant with a long leaf on it, and the morning dew was still clinging to its leaves. So as we were walking along I would grab these leaves and start licking the moisture off them. Everybody else started copying me. It left a peculiar taste in the mouth, a tang off the leaf, but it did manage to quench our thirst.

When we complained, the major in charge of the middle of the column, who spoke a little bit of English, tried to impose a different system on us. That was at our first lunch break. He had soggy boiled rice prepared for us.

'You will eat this,' he said, 'then you will not need to drink more water till tonight.'

'It is not possible,' we answered.

'Yes, it is possible.' He explained: 'UNITA are trained this way. You eat the rice and your stomach absorbs the water out of the rice into your system, so you don't need water. Just because your throat is dry it doesn't mean to say you are thirsty.'

'He's got different ways of interpreting a thirst,' I muttered to John. But there was something in what he said, of course.

On the third morning when we halted for the lunch break after about six hours, we stopped by a river, and there we took a bath, our first wash for three days. It was beautiful. All the rivers in that part of Angola that we walked over are crystal-clear. You could look down into a stream seven or eight feet deep and see the pebbles on the bottom and freshwater weeds waving in the water. Some of the rivers were just like liquid glass, with a very faint tint of brown – the peat – at the bottom. And that water was, as it turned out, delicious to drink.

That was the occasion of my first set-to with the Portuguese. They had not understood what I said about saving the beer cans; but they should have used their brains a bit. Barely had we set out again on the second leg of the day's march when they were demanding water from the Filipinos.

That was it. I climbed into them.

'The bloody brook is down there. You go and drink your fill now,' I said. 'When you are thirsty, maybe in two or three hours' time, then you ask for a drink. But not before.'

'The Filipinos are not on the same standard as us,' they were saying. 'They must give way to us.'

'No way, mister,' I said. 'In the first place, they don't work for you, they work for me. In the second place, everybody here is on equal standard, regardless of nationality.'

That didn't go down too well. The electrician started getting a bit cocky, and I told him to eff off.

'I understand that word "eff off",' he said.

'Good,' I replied. 'Now eff off.'

He was getting all uppity, wanting to stick one on me.

'If you put one finger on me, my friend,' I said, 'I will break your neck.'

I don't think it would have come to fisticuffs. He was just having a go, and he backed off. But it was true that, now we were captives, law and order and civilized ways of behaviour were disintegrating and we were reverting to an animal state where we were ready to fight for what we wanted, or to defend what we had got.

Quite a few times I got my claws out to do battle. I think the closest it ever came to a fight was one night between me and Bushbunny. We were coming off a march, on a hillside somewhere, and had dropped our blankets on the ground and just fallen down asleep on to them. I had half a bottle of milk, powdered milk, which UNITA had given me because I had diarrhoea. He had been collecting wood, and he came up and threw all this wood down right against my head. I looked up and told him: 'Watch it, Bushbunny, just watch it.'

He went off again, collected another armful of wood and threw it on top of the heap, which knocked this bottle of milk over.

'One more crack,' I said, 'and that is your lot.'

He went off and got another armful, which he dropped right next to my head. It hit me; and that was it, I was up and at him. I got him by the throat and I was really going to put one on him, because all the tensions from the past few days were coming to the surface. I think I would have knocked his head off. John came up behind me and grabbed my arm as I held Bushbunny by the windpipe. I squeezed his windpipe and tried to lift him off his feet. He was kicking and trying to scream. But as John had my arm, I just threw him back. It was a good thing that I didn't fight because I might have lost some of the respect of the Filipinos, by descending to animal level (though I should add that all the Filipinos were urging me on; they were cheering and clapping and dancing around).

The Filipinos did not like the Portuguese, and in particular they did not like Bushbunny. That was common to all of us, and it was partly because the Portuguese did better than we did, and of the Portuguese Bushbunny did best of all. For though the Angolans hated the Portuguese in general, in practice they had been used to doing things for them, under their orders or at their request, and the Portuguese with us gradually worked up a friendly relationship with the UNITA lads. They would even have some of them running around for them, and getting them tobacco. And of all the Portuguese Bushbunny did by far the best. He had years of experience of cadging and chatting up behind him in his life as a hobo. He always managed to get extra food, always managed to come back with a piece of goat that had meat on, or manioca, or corn on the cob, when we couldn't get any. We would try and try, but he always succeeded where others failed. And this made him particularly detested – even more by the Filipinos, most of whom, unlike us, could speak Portuguese and so had a way of communicating with the cooks and soldiers that we did not have.

Not that the Portuguese were the only ones who tried to exploit the Filipinos. Even John used to say: 'You don't tell a Filipino what to do. You demand that he does it.'

'No,' I would answer to him, 'a lot depends on the character of the Filipino. Some I will ask to do something, some I will tell to do something, and some I will demand to do something. It is all according to the individual.'

But John confined himself, at worst, to ordering them about. It was the Captain who really set about . . . not exactly robbing them, but diddling them out of their fair shares. He was a most selfish man. I had quite a few slanging matches with him. Al could never say anything against him; but we could – and we did. His selfishness didn't bother me personally but it bothered me when it came to the Filipinos. That really got on my nelly.

On one occasion on the march my feet were crippled. They were about twice their normal size, septic, and agony to put on the floor. That particular day we stopped about 2 p.m., and we were shattered. I told the Filipinos: 'It doesn't matter how sick you are, always take your biscuits.'

We used to get two biscuits each every day. There were six Filipinos down with acute vomiting and diarrhoea, but even then I told them: 'It doesn't matter: take your biscuits, because you can save them and eat them later.'

I had a piece of thin curtain and I used to put it over my face so that I could sleep, or doze, because I couldn't sleep with flies on my face. We were all crashed out under these trees and just dozing when we heard the Captain's voice:

'You give me those biscuits.'

I threw off the curtain and sat up. He had a fistful of biscuits. This one lad was lying down with his biscuits on his chest, and the Captain was trying to open his fingers to get them. I got up and I hobbled over and kicked him straight in the arse. I was in agony. I hopped around holding my foot for about an hour. The tears were running from my eyes – it was that painful. But I am really glad I kicked him. He had gone round five Filipinos and had just taken the biscuits; never asked for them, just taken them. That was the kind of man he was. And that was the kind of people the Filipinos were. It is their nature not to protest. They are very soft.

After this I told them many a time: 'As soon as you get your biscuits, put them inside you or inside your pockets, whichever, out of sight.' And we needed those biscuits, all of us: for the diarrhoea came, though not immediately, when we drank stream water. It really hit us later on when we were in lower country, down from the hills.

It was a real night march that carried us through that Monday 31 December, into the New Year. We had acquired a notebook that must have fallen out of one of UNITA's backpacks, and Paul and John (but mainly Paul) kept it up alternately day by day from then on. Paul wrote of that night: '*We all slept a little in the early evening. Then we were woken at 9.30 p.m. and the walking began again.*'

As a matter of fact this means that we must have been asleep when the BBC's six o'clock news first reported in the UK that we had been taken hostage. If Lynn was thinking of me, I was certainly thinking of her, and the girls, too. As Paul went on: '*We thought about the folks at home celebrating with food and drink. By now we are really beginning to long for the bare essentials: tea, coffee, beer, cigarettes, chicken vindaloo, etc. But no chance for some time yet. At about 11.45 p.m. GMT we sat in a gully, rain pouring down, surrounded by UNITA troops, tired and wet. We wished each other "Happy New Year" and celebrated with a damp cigarette between the four of us. As we walked on it was pitch black. We had had no real sleep for 72 hours and we suffered hallucinations.'*

That night we continued walking into 1985 till long past dawn, not halting till 8 a.m. They were pushing us really hard and the pace didn't ease off as we had been promised. It never really did ease off till we reached Jamba.

Paul, as the diary shows, hadn't yet come to terms with being captured and all it entailed. For the first day he had been in total shock. When he was first brought into the group from the aircraft he was as white as a sheet and he was shaking. He wasn't used to deprivations or to living rough. Another thing that probably weighed on him at first was the fact that this other lad of 22, this Filipino called Philip, the one who had clung to me like a leech when we were captured, was now doing better on the march than Paul was. Paul was trying to show that he wasn't bothered, but he was. It wasn't until he realized that the rest of us *were* bothered and weren't too proud to show it that he felt he could relax, ease off a bit, show his feelings and accept the problems. But those first few days we had to explain everything to him calmly: how he would have to do this, how he would have to do that. It is very difficult for any young lad to have a bunch of hooligans – black, too – ordering him about. He just could not accept that at first.

As for myself, I had never been under the control of black people before; and at first I found it a bit humiliating because in my fifteen-odd years overseas I had always been in a position where I was in control of blacks, not *vice versa*. On the other hand I have always had a good working relationship with black people, and I get on well with them. I couldn't work in Africa if I didn't. Funnily enough – this is probably hard for a lot of people to believe – when you are working with blacks in Africa, you don't think of them as black or coloured, you simply regard them as individuals and accept them as they are.

So after we were captured by UNITA, we resented it quite strongly at first when it really hit us that black guys were in charge of us. 'Are they going to manage it o.k.?' we wondered. But later, as time went by and we realized that they were doing the best they could for us, we would just accept everything they said without quibbling. Indeed, when they told us to do things, we would do whatever it was straight away without thinking about it, without any resentment at all at their being blacks giving orders to whites.

The only people we did resent were individuals whom we would have resented whatever the colour of their skin. The one we resented most was the lieutenant directly in charge of the hostages. Lieutenant Potash was his name; but he was always yelling and bawling, so we called him Gob. He would come up behind us and shout '*Vam, vam, vam*' – 'Go, go, go' – and '*Docka, docka, docka*' – 'Faster, faster, faster'.

Personally I would slag this guy. I would stop in my tracks and turn round when he came up behind me and did this '*Docka, docka*'. I would throw every vile word I could think of at him and he would look blank because he couldn't understand a thing I was saying. It was childish, really. But he got the general gist – and I felt great afterwards.

Captain Cat, who commanded the rear of the column, was a tall, thin guy, an interesting character. He spoke moderate English and we could get some points through to him. He occasionally informed us of the correct time, GMT, and he told us that he liked the BBC. He had some knowledge of London and the UK.

He was a genuine person but I had, personally, to keep a wary eye on him because he had designs on my hat. Above its peak it carried the letters CAT – short for Caterpillar, the heavy plant company. This bloke did everything he could to get my hat. First he tried bribery – tobacco – but I wasn't giving up my protection from the sun, even for cigarettes. When that failed, he'd send his lads up during the night to try and steal the hat. But I always used it as a sort of pillowcase over my shoes, and rested my head on it, so that didn't work either. He never did get that CAT hat, much though he desired it!

Up at the head of the column was Major Usabious. He had a high-powered hunting rifle, but he was not an actual fighting man. He was in the engineers, the man who built the bridges and did the path-finding. We did not see him often or have much contact with him, which was a pity as he spoke English and was a very pleasant character. Also he was the only one of all the officers who would tell the truth. The others – we would ask them 'How much farther?' and they would say 'Ten minutes more.' Ten minutes would drag into an hour, and we would ask again: 'How long before we stop?' 'Oh, two more hours,' they would say – and that would be four hours. But Major Usabious was always accurate.

The other major – we never did get his name clear – was in charge of the whole party and could usually be found moving up and down the centre of the column. He was a small man but he had an air of authority. He seemed to be cool and confident, and he spoke a little English. He told us that this was his area; and, after the departure of the lieutenant colonel (we never did see him again), this major was in command of the whole battalion.

These three officers each had a radio operator who used to walk behind them, and thus they would communicate from the head to the tail of the column by walkie-talkie. The sets were American, with power-packs, strapped to the chests and backs of the operators, and they worked reasonably efficiently. The radio operators also had to carry hand generators that they would crank by hand to recharge the power-packs, and sometimes we would hear them winding these things all night.

The walkie-talkies had a range of about three miles. The battalion also had one long-range radio, for communication with headquarters. It was top secret and we were never allowed near it, but we could see it in action occasionally. The aerial had to be thrown high up into the trees, and while the radio operator tuned in his assistant had to pedal a sort of bicycle to keep the batteries charged.

The major had one star, a green beret, a crown, green tabs. He had a backpack in which he kept his maps and notebooks, and a Portuguese pistol. He and the other officers were armed with a deluxe-type AK with a walnut butt on it and a polished magazine case. They wore sand-brown leather belts, khaki jungle-type camouflage jacket and trousers and deep red boots. Captain Cat wore a black peak cap with no marks on; but I think he was out of order. Lieutenant Potash, to give him his due, was smart at all times; even when he was ragged, he was still smart; he was that sort of guy.

The discipline was good. If the major gave an order to Captain Cat, he would turn round and salute him and obey. If the men wanted to talk to an officer, they would go up and salute and ask permission. If they were walking by, and the major was standing at the side of the track, they wouldn't salute but they would straighten up. Then when they had passed him they would go back to the slog again. It was a complete contrast to the slap-happy FAPLAs we had known in Cafunfo. And these lads really grafted. This was a total surprise to us because it was unlike anything we had been used to in Angola before; we had simply never known anything like it.

Mind you, officers apart, the troops were really tatty. This was hardly surprising because some of them had been in the field two years and were due to go back to Jamba for rest, rehabilitation and retraining. But what did surprise me was the state of their weapons. They had these Belgian FNs, captured from the Portuguese – old, rusty, with bits chipped out of them, badly neglected. Some of them I would not have liked to try and shoot with at all because the barrels were bent.

They never looked after their equipment. Indeed, whenever they tripped over, their tendency was to throw their weapons aside so that they did not land on them. Twice I was caught like that. The first time, walking down a slope, this pillock next to me fell over. His rifle barrel went between my legs, and I went flat on my face. I was so mad, I picked up his rifle and threw it into the bush – and he had to go and fetch it, which he did without a word. The second time, at night, a guy fell over in front of me, dropping his bazooka, and again it went between my legs and had me on my face. This may all sound a bit trivial, but because of the foot problem it was not: any fall really increased the agony, and by the end of the first stage of the march we were all in agony. As Paul wrote in the diary (and this time I utterly agree with him): '*These days have merged into a period of thirst, hunger and pain. At times we have stumbled along in a state of semi-consciousness. I don't think any of us will ever forget the experience.*'

Paul, in fact, did comparatively well because he had Doc Martin boots, which proved excellent for marching in and never gave him any problems. But I had these town boots, as they call them, with a high, 1-inch heel. When I was walking on the flat it was not bad, and when I was walking uphill it was even better. But on steep slopes, downhill – and there were many of these – I would land on my heels and the toes would not touch the ground because the foot simply did not stretch that far.

These were old boots, with a cardboard sole inside the

shoe; and what with my feet sweating and the wet weather, this sole disintegrated almost immediately. From the heel to the sole ran a steel strip, held in place by two self-tapping screws, which stopped the shoe bending in the middle. One of these screws worked loose on the second day of the march and punched a hole in my heel – though it wasn't till we stopped and I took my boot off that I found this screw sticking out.

So I ripped a piece off my blanket and shoved it into my boot to try and give my foot some protection. The trouble was that this made the foot tight inside the boot; and in the swamps – squelch, squelch for hours, up to the knees in wet – the piece of blanket held the water. It just would not dry out. This meant that the skin on my feet became very, very soft and of course it started to break and split.

In the swamps, mixed with this black peat, were very fine grains of black sand that would get into the broken flesh. The flesh wound would start to heal up with the black sand inside; the result was that it would then turn septic. I had seven holes gouged into my right foot, and five into my left foot. On my left foot the heel bone was showing.

Once a day the UNITA medic used to come round and treat our feet. He would scrape out the blisters with a hot spoon where they had gone septic or had festered, and pour in this red iodine stuff that I have already mentioned. It stung like Jesus. It killed you, this stuff, when he poured it in. But though it worked at first, once I was back in the swamps my wounds would fester and turn septic once more.

With my feet swelling up, I was unable, at times, even to get my boots on, and I would try walking without them. That was agony. The paths UNITA use are very narrow; they walk in single file by lifting one foot up, swinging it in front of the other one and then putting it down in the same line. The result, rather than a path, is a little trench in the ground about 5½-6 inches wide and, depending on how much use it has had, about 2 inches deep. The grass grows over this trench-path so that from the air it cannot be spotted. But if – as happened – my foot ever got stuck in this sodding trench, over I would go; there was just no way of keeping one's balance. And if I gave up and walked on the side, the UNITA lads would scream and shout at me, because of the tell-tale signs I might leave for air reconnaissance.

In the areas of dense bush there would be little stumps of

trees, about ½ inch round and sticking up ½ inch above the earth, along these trench-paths. When I hit these with my toe or my heel the shock would go right through me and explode in my brain. By this time I was barefoot or wearing what was left of my boots: the heels were flapping off by then and the strip of metal in one of the boots had broken – it was unendurable. That is the only word for it . . . unendurable. Even now, thinking back, it gives me the shudders.

By this stage even UNITA were becoming exhausted, and having trouble with their own feet. The medic himself had a monstrous blister on the sole of his foot behind his big toe. There we were squealing and grunting with pain, and there was this poor sucker with this great hole in the sole of his foot; and yet he was walking.

One of the young cook girls went down with foot problems too. I remember that she had been limping for quite a while and had been bandaged up. We were going up a steep slope past a river when we heard this screaming coming from the trees ahead. As we zigzagged up this slope, we went past her. No wonder she was screaming the place down. I don't quite know what was happening but the medic was hacking into the top of her foot with something like a jack knife. All the same, about an hour later she overtook us. Her foot must have been hanging in shreds.

I think the only explanation is that UNITA took marijuana, and that was one of the things that kept them going. I think they used to chew it. They never offered us any, but, to be quite honest, if they had I would have accepted it, and I would have used it. It would have saved a lot of aggravation – especially as by this time we were getting to the stage where sheer misery was overcoming our fear. We had not expected such harsh treatment. We had been told that four or five days' hard marching would bring us out of FAPLA territory, and then we could ease off. But in those first days of January they kept pushing us on – over 20 miles every day – and we started bucking a bit, swearing at them, that sort of thing. All of us did this, Europeans and Americans alike – except for the Captain. The disappointing thing about him, for an airline captain, was that he would not take any responsibility; he would not help us fight for anything. He was always a background man; he wouldn't give advice to anybody. The Filipinos were in dire straits, too, but unlike the rest of us he would not chivvy them along or do anything to help. He would just plod on his way and sod everything else – including Al, who was his fellow-American and crew member. About this time he told Al that a helicopter would soon be picking them up as UNITA dare not hold Americans hostage (it never came).

By the Friday – that's to say six days after his capture – Al was fading rapidly. I think we all thought that he would not make it in those first few days because he was such a physical wreck to start with. He was overweight; he also had palpitations and was taking tablets for his heart condition. Furthermore, he had accidentally burnt his socks on the very first night. That was a disaster. The socks were wet and he was trying to dry them over the fire and they just caught, burning the foot out of his sock. After that it was flesh direct on to the boot, and that was what started his blisters off.

At the same time he had made another mistake. He was wearing flying-boots and he had slit them, after he lost the nail off his small toe, because they were too tight across the toes. The trouble was that the swamp mud would infiltrate through this slot and fill his boots with black slime, which turned the blisters septic. Under his big toe the ligaments had come off everything and there was just a raw hole. He was in agony. So what with his feet being in a terrible way and his general condition being so bad he just collapsed with exhaustion.

It had been a particularly bad day that Friday, with torrential rain all the way. We were crossing open plains without any shelter and were all desperately tired. We were at the end of our tether.

Then, at 2 p.m., after seven hours' forced marching, we limped into a base camp. It was unreal. UNITA girls came flocking out to sing us a welcome song. They sang and danced for us for about an hour: a welcome song, a liberation song, songs in Portuguese, and so on. There were some beautiful girls among them. They had nice dresses, or blouses and skirts, good bras and pants, a lot of nice stuff. Down to the knees you would have a beautiful girl singing and dancing; and that was fine as long as you stopped at the knees. But if your eyes wandered down to the feet, then all was spoilt: for there would be a big pair of military boots, a couple of clodhoppers going clonk, clonk, clonk. That really spoilt them. Even in Jamba we never saw a girl with a nice feminine pair of shoes on.

We were taken to a river to wash, and we were even given some scented soap. It was perfect, though we wished we could have cleaned our teeth too. Then we went up to the camp where the major issued us with a couple of home-made cigarettes each, and we crashed out inside huts on grass beds raised on stilts. Beautiful it was, the first decent night's kip. And what was even better was that the next day, the Saturday, was a holiday, a day of total rest for us. It was exactly a week now since Cafunfo had fallen and we had been taken hostage. We were told by the major that the radio had announced our capture, and that our families knew we were alive and safe.

The high point of that holiday was the appearance of a UNITA general, followed by a rally. This was our first rally, but they all adopted the same programme. It was propaganda, really, and each rally would last about two hours in all. A woman from every different province of Angola would come forward and make a short speech about her particular state. It was all in Portuguese and we couldn't understand a word, though – as John put it in the diary – '*the depth of feeling in the people was plainly evident*'. The speeches went on for about half an hour, then they would have singing, soldiers on one side and girls on the other, chanting in unison, then alternatively and with a descant. Then there were more speeches, with applause and cries of '*Viva la UNITA!*' and everyone going 'Ya ya ya, yayaya' – a typical Third World political demonstration.

After the rally the general's wife came up and presented us with a cake specially baked for us, a belated New Year's presentation, and that cake was certainly the high point of *our* day. It was very nice, a real morale-booster. The general's wife was not your average Angolan. She had a bit of class. She walked and talked differently. She even spoke a little bit of English. She was nothing like the girls who had been looking after us on the march.

When we pulled in to the base camp and the major told us we were going to be there for twenty-four hours, these girls came round and demanded all our clothes. We had to strip right off and cover ourselves in a blanket. Some of the Filipinos were slow, so the girls chivvied them and even started pulling their trousers down. At first we could not make out what they were after. It was all very businesslike. In fact, they simply wanted to launder our clothes, to wash them in the river and, as time was short, to have them laid out to dry as quickly as possible. In all we were probably to have our clothes laundered four or five times. It was well organized – no two ways about it.

This particular time, though, as our clothes were so torn, they issued us with a new shirt and a new pair of socks each. These were thick nylon socks and the trouble with them was that they tended to hold sand. When, after a white sand patch, we went through a swamp, we would find we were walking on a layer of sand bedded into the socks – uncomfortable at the best of times, but agony with blisters.

They also issued some of us with long trousers. As I said earlier, I don't like long trousers and I always wear shorts in Africa. But as a result my legs during the week's marching had been pretty ripped up. The thorns I had not minded so much, because the thorns were hip height and would rip my shorts rather than my legs. But the really difficult time had been going through the long grass, where the blades would slice deep. That had been hard-going.

So I accepted the long trousers – though I was to regret it afterwards. I tried them on, and they were a bit too small for me, very tight under the crutch. But, I thought, I will lose weight and very soon they will be a perfect fit. What was really on my mind was my shoes.

'Major,' I said, 'there is no way I can walk any more with these shoes. They are finished.'

I showed him the shoes, and I showed him my feet. Even the medic told him there was no way I could go on with them. I had been hoping for a pair of military boots, but as this was an attack battalion they had none to spare. Indeed, not all of their own men had boots. There was one UNITA trooper who had simply one wellington – and if you have ever walked any distance in wellingtons yourself, you will know that this is about the worst footwear there could be for blisters. But this lad, though he was carrying about 45-50 lbs in weight, would not throw his one welly away. It must have been his most precious possession. After we had been through a swamp, we could hear him for hours afterwards: squelch, squelch, squelch. He was with us for about three weeks with this one welly. But for myself there was no chance of military boots, the major explained. He seemed to take my point about the condition of my feet, but he just nodded and went away.

By this time we were getting philosophical. We were just living from day to day and making the best of things. So, though I ought to have been, I wasn't too worried. I counted my blessings – I was still alive, my family knew it, and I knew they knew – and made the best of it while I could.

Chapter V

The Long March: 2

Indeed it was amazing what a single day's rest, and the cake, had done for our morale. I would not say we were exactly raring to go the following morning; but in one way we wanted to get on with it now, to get it over with. 'Twenty days to Jamba,' we were saying to each other.

'It is a fantastic city, Jamba,' UNITA was telling us. 'There is electric light and everything you want. There are showers, steel beds with mattresses, everything.' So already Jamba was to us like a crock of gold at the end of the rainbow.

But personally I still had this immediate problem with my boots, and nothing had been done about it. So, when they were getting us out of the huts ready to march, I just sat down.

'Come, we must go, we must go to Jamba,' they said.

I refused to move.

'I need something for my feet,' I insisted.

Eventually they called the major, and he hadn't forgotten the problem; he came up with a pair of high-heeled cowboy boots, size 5 (I take 8½s), and a pair of plastic sandals. Bushbunny, whose shoes had also collapsed and who had very small feet, took the cowboy boots – later he shaved the heels off to avoid the problem I had had – and I took the plastic sandals.

So off we went, heading east-south-east this time, and the sandals felt comfortable. The soles were good and strong and whenever I put my foot down on one of those stumps in the trench-path the sandals spread the weight out, which the boots had never done. It wasn't till I had been going two or three hours that I realized that they had their disadvantages too. They were open-toed. So if there was a stick lying on a path, it would go straight through my sock and in between my toes. If the stick was fixed firmly in the ground, it was particularly agonizing. Many a time I would pick straw up too; and then I would hop along, trying to pull it out, trying to keep up.

But it was an easy day's march, that first day of the second stage, and we had only done about five miles when we stopped for lunch. The way we kept a count of the distances we had done was this: we would take it in turns, counting each stride on one leg, ignoring the stride on the other, estimating one stride at one yard. We would time ourselves over each 1000 yards and every day we would check our timing over a 1000-yard stretch. If we were marching uphill, still maintaining the same time, we would knock off half a mile. Some days we would walk faster and some days we would walk slower but generally speaking it was a pretty accurate reckoning, and we kept it up right from the beginning. That first week, for instance, we reckoned we had done 6 miles on the day we were captured, then 21, then 23 – that was the full night's march, and a record for the whole trip – and then 18 miles per day after that.

Our main problem in the days that followed was the food, as the tinned stuff that UNITA had looted at Cafunfo was beginning to run out. The first thing to go off the menu was the tinned milk. It was sickly sweet, but it had been a real luxury because it had given us the energy to go on, and we had taken it gladly. Then the powdered milk and the sugar and the rest of the tinned stuff ran out too. So they turned to the goats: a lot of goats had been captured at Cafunfo and herded along the trail with us.

But we hostages always seemed to get the tail-end of the goat meat. Once I was given a goat's jawbone, complete with teeth, which had just a little bit of meat on the side. On another occasion I had a foot with the fur still on it, broken off beneath the joint; and on another a piece of lung. One thing I could not eat was a bit of windpipe about three inches long. I was holding this thing between my finger and thumb and it was wobbling about in the breeze like a jelly.

'Do you expect me to eat this?' I asked the major.

'You don't want it?' he asked.

'No way,' I replied.

He simply snatched it out of my hand and swallowed it. You might say that was greed. I would say it was leadership.

The only time we ever got ribs was if they killed a kid that had just been born and could not keep up. These ribs were dinky little things, two ribs together only half an inch wide, and about 1½ inches long; and there was no meat on them. Only once did I ever get a nice piece of meat, and I can still remember now the pleasure that gave me. It had been fried, and it was absolutely delicious.

One particular area we went through was cultivated – and this was a rarity, because that whole stretch of Angola seemed to be almost uninhabited. But here there were millions and millions of corn on the cob. What the UNITA cook girls did then was to strip the corn off the cob, grind it into a powder and dry it so that they could carry it. Then they would mix it into a paste with warm water and give us this for our meals.

The first time we had this they added a surprise: they had been keeping a precious tin of corned beef in reserve. They mixed that in, added a lot of water, and the result was like a weak gravy, nice, a different sort of taste, quite edible. But we kept getting this stuff, and, as it got older, we started to find sand in it and bits of grass, even the odd toe nail and things like that; it put us right off. Occasionally, by way of contrast, we had corn on the cob raw; we used to roast that for ourselves on the fire at night. But a meal would consist of one corn on the cob only between the three of us.

Our staple food, however, was funge. It had a twang to it and it looked revolting. It reminded us of grey wallpaper paste and we had it day in, day out.

Funge is made from manioca, which is a root crop; each vegetable is about as big as a swede, long and tapered. The cook girls would take it out of the earth, peel it, cut it into small slices and then lay it on the ground to dry in the sun. (If it is left unsliced, it starts to ferment within three days.) When it was dry, they would pound it into a powder, and then the UNITA lads would sack it up. When the time came to make a meal, they would mix it with warm water. That was it. Personally I have eaten funge under civilized conditions in people's houses, when it was like a pure white dough, tasteless but quite pleasant, particularly with spices added. But this stuff, though it started off as a white powder, became a grey-brown paste when mixed with water – probably because it had not been dry enough when pounded up.

For myself, even when I was absolutely starving I could only eat about three or four spoonfuls of this stuff. Then I would gag on the next and throw it back up. I would try and put my mind on something else and continue to swallow it, but I could feel the muscles in my stomach contracting, ready to throw it back out again. The Captain would eat it; he would manage to get little red peppers to spice his funge with. John and Paul both hated it, but they could manage to eat it. John, as

I said before, had this high metabolism: he burnt off energy, and he had to eat, however much he was revolted, to keep himself going.

But Al was like myself. He could not eat it. Al and I would eat as much as we could, then we would leave it for ten minutes or so before trying again. We might get one more mouthful down. Alternatively we would try to disguise the taste. For example, we would mash the thing into a ball and hold it on sticks over the fire, trying to bake it. But it was even more revolting that way.

So even a tiny little bit of goat meat to chew on made all the difference. The UNITA catering corps (as we baptized them) with the battalion consisted of about 18-20 cook girls whose job was to cook for us and for the officers, and generally to look after us. They used to march along, each with a pile of plates or mugs, or perhaps a cooking pot, wrapped in a bedsheet and balanced high on their heads. The youngest of them would be about 12 or 13 and the oldest about 25. When we halted, the girls would swing into action. They would unload, go off and get water (that would usually take about half an hour), fetch wood and so on while the cook boy got the cooking fire going. Then, if we were having goat, they would kill a goat by shattering it with an axe (there were no knives at all), strip it out and start cooking.

The food would be dished out pretty evenly, on aluminium plates. In the early days, when we were fit, we would stand up to try and see which plate had the most meat on it – like a shattered knuckle joint, for instance. But later on in the march there was just no way we had the energy to stand up and see what was on the plates.

Then the girls would bring containers round and we would fill our cans up with water. What we would have done without those beer cans I have no idea. They were very flimsy and sometimes you would hear one of the Filipinos cursing because he had turned over in the night, lain on his can and flattened it.

After the meal the girls would come back and collect the plates, and then wash the dishes in the nearest stream. As I have said, they did our laundry at the long halts and they would show us down to the streams when we were allowed to wash. The girls would always be upstream, and we always managed to get next to the girls so that we would only have their muck passed down to us. Below us there would be maybe as many as

60 or 70 UNITA troops standing washing themselves or doing whatever. We would try to be modest and turn our backs on the girls while we were washing, but they did not give a damn. They would finish washing themselves and then come out and sit on the bank combing their hair out and laughing and looking at us. They were peculiar girls and they had a queer attitude for African women, who are usually modest; but I suppose they had been in the bush that long, it just didn't bother them.

One of these cook girls – she was about 18 or 19 – had a modern corselette with the stocking straps and the lace at the front. Indeed, most of the girls had oddments of dress that the soldiers had looted somewhere and that they had given these girls as a favour. But this particular girl, she would come and dish our dinner up with this lace thing on. We would whistle at her and make the odd remark, and she would giggle.

It never went any further than that. They all slept in a group, and there was one in charge of them, the matron as it were, who looked after the girls. If too many soldiers came around, she would chase them off. She dogged everybody. All the same, seeing that the battalion had been in the bush for seven or eight months, there was quite a bit of caution going on between the cook girls and the soldiers. There was the occasional illicit love affair, but without the matron's knowledge, I am sure of that. There were no babies around – though later on, between two base camps, we did pick up some women carrying kids of six or seven months old in their arms. They were probably soldiers' wives on the move; they did no cooking for us or anything else of that nature.

The UNITA soldiers, I should explain, cooked for themselves. They would gather in groups of three or four men around a hundred little fires. The smoke would puther out of the bush and could be seen for miles. If for any reason – because, for instance, we were approaching FAPLA territory and there was fear of FAPLA helicopter gunships – orders were given that no fires were to be lit, they would eat raw cassava, which didn't taste bad.

They also kept going on manioca brew, the local alcohol. On the second day of this stage Al had collapsed. Everyone else had carried on and gone ahead but I stayed behind with Al. We managed to scrounge some tobacco off a soldier to roll a cigarette with. Before we had been captured, it had always been the Angolans who would try and beg cigarettes off us. We would turn them down and tell them to sod off. Now the roles were completely reversed because it was we that were doing the begging. To come down to the nitty-gritty, we had lost some of our pride just to keep our smoking habit going. Thinking about it now, Gordon Bennett! that was degrading.

Anyway, Al and I were sitting there having a smoke when Captain Cat and his men came up.

'You have got to get going,' he kept saying. But Al was in no condition.

'It is only down the valley and up the other side,' he explained.

He was always saying that sort of thing. We would think to ourselves: I doubt I can make it even to the other side of the valley. Then, at the other side of the valley, it would be 'just to the next ridge', and that might be six miles away, just a blue haze in the distance.

We usually obeyed, but this time he couldn't get us to our feet. Then he had an idea.

'Would some beer do you any good?' he asked.

'Yes, definitely,' I said, thinking, 'The crafty sod! He still has a can or two of Beck's tucked away.'

But instead he poured this white liquid out.

'What is this?' I asked, suspicious.

'Manioca alcohol,' he replied.

Al was game for anything, even if it was the dreaded funge in another form, and so was I; so we tried this. There was a real tang to it, not unpleasant. We drank what had been poured out for us, then he gave us some more, and we drank that too. I was a bit tiddly; and walking down that valley and up the other side didn't then seem to matter a damn to me. We were hoping for some more, but that was the last we ever saw, which was a shame because it could have dulled quite a few problems and relieved the monotony.

I was fed up with the monotony of walking – we all were – but it was Paul who really suffered from boredom. I was not bored at all, not on the march. I could think about lots of different things – the past, the present, and what I wanted to do in the future – that is, when I wasn't being forced to concentrate on my feet. But Paul's feet were in good condition and it was just the sheer monotony for him. Also, I don't think Paul found it easy to occupy his mind; it was a question of different mentalities. He needed something happening around him, someone to talk to, some stimulus. But when he was walking he was virtually alone because the man in front wasn't talking and the man behind wasn't talking. Without continual conversation Paul had a tendency to sink into depression.

Now and again on the march we would talk across each other's shoulders or to the back of the man in front. But it didn't last long. We might mention a beautiful valley, trees or flowers, just that sort of talk. Even when we came to the end of a day's march, and were eating or sitting around, we did not say much. We just did not have the energy to talk.

The people who really kept cheerful were the Filipinos. Sometimes we would arrive at the camping site, shattered, at 2 a.m., as we did that particular night, and everybody would have their orders or things to do: unload, collect wood and so on. But once the fires were started everybody would sit down; and round the Filipinos' fires we would hear the jokes being cracked. It would usually start with Francis: he was the one who could wind them up. He would have them giggling and then within a few minutes they would all be laughing and cracking off. They were a happy bunch, considering the circumstances they were in.

Major Usabious, as I mentioned earlier, was in charge of the trail-finding. He carried an exercise book in his pack and once when we had a break I sat down just a little behind him to one side, and I looked over his shoulder as he was studying this. All it showed was trails, where they met other trails, and the different signs on the different trails.

I didn't twig it at first, because at first we had been on this road out of Cafunfo where there was obviously no need for signs. But thereafter every trail had signs cut into trees, probably about a mile or even two miles apart, along its route. The first sign I had noticed cut into a tree was an oblong, and it was an odd-looking sign, easy to miss, because the bark had grown in. Later on it changed to a triangle. Then there were two oblong slots; and on the next long trail it was a square. These signs weren't exactly on the side of the trails, they were probably 20-30 feet off – only visible if you were really looking for them. When we came to a plain, as we left the bush there would be one of these signs and as we re-entered the bush on the far side of the plain, we would pick up a tree with another.

That was basically how UNITA found its way across country; and it needed a lot of expertise. But the surprising thing was that there were only two occasions when there was fumbling and we had to backtrack – though this did show the seriousness of losing one's way, because on one of these two occasions we had to backtrack for half a day.

Major Usabious was also in charge of the bridge-building. It was now Tuesday 6 January, eleven days after our capture, and we halted while he built a bridge.

What UNITA used to do was to construct underwater bridges which could not be spotted from the air. These would consist of two parallel logs about 12 inches in diameter sunk into either bank, but below the waterline. Most bridges were already in position along the trails; but occasionally one might have been washed away, or it might be a new trail and a new crossing needing a new bridge. This particular river was about 15 feet wide and about 10-12 feet deep, crystal clear but with a very strong current flowing. So it was quite a long job for Major Usabious' men to get the logs the right length and properly in position, anchored in the banks and exactly parallel, two feet apart, against the strong flow of the current. There was no handrail, so you just had to go down on hands and knees and crawl across slowly, concentrating on keeping your balance. Luckily not one of us fell in. Major Usabious chatted with us as we were waiting for the bridge to be constructed. He assured us that our names had been released by UNITA and that our families knew we were alive and safe. He was a thoughtful man. He asked us to write to him when we got back to England. But none of us ever did.

Next day Paul managed to scrounge a whole mealie – that is what the South Africans call corn on the cob – and the day afterwards a tin of sardines. These were so much the high points that John noted them in the diary. But then Paul went and left this tin of sardines, which we were holding in reserve, behind where we had slept. He simply forgot it, the pillock!

Meanwhile I had other worries. Agostino, the Portuguese electrician, was showing signs of malaria: in fact, he was to suffer from two bouts on the trail, though like all the Portuguese he managed to keep marching the whole way; as regards the marching, they were tough – you have to give them that. Then the following night I started shivering and shaking and thought I was going down with the same thing. They gave me some hot milk and sugar – they had been keeping a special reserve for cases of malaria. I managed to sleep. And when I woke up I was o.k. – good luck was with me.

The next thing that struck was diarrhoea – which was a good thing for John, who (as Paul put it in the diary) '*celebrated the breaking of his constipation record today with a grand total of fifteen days without so much as a touch of wind*'. But it was definitely a bad thing for the rest of us, demoralizing and very weakening. We were at a much lower altitude now, coming down from the hills, and the water was much dirtier. Vomiting struck us as well, and the slightest scratch became infected, because what with poor diet and exhaustion our natural immunities were weakened.

At the very same time tension was beginning to build up among UNITA, because we were approaching the asphalt road, the main link between Luanda on the west coast and FAPLA's big base at Saurimo, about 120 miles from Angola's eastern border. We knew that this was heavily patrolled and the main problem was that the road ran through an open plain, so we would be out in the open for about a mile leading up to the road and about half a mile once we were across it. As we neared the end of the bush, UNITA started abandoning the single-file system and splitting up into columns.

At this stage I knew, for the first time, exactly where we were: 42½ miles from Kapenda in the west, and probably 108-120 miles from Saurimo in the east. I knew that if I could get away I would eventually be picked up by a FAPLA convoy. I was even confident that I could, once I had escaped, make my own way through the bush (which would have been safer*) for about a week or ten days till I reached Kapenda. If I had been alone, I think I would have gone. But at this stage I felt even more responsible for the Filipinos than I had at the start of the march; and their condition was beginning to deteriorate. Cookie, for instance, had developed a big boil on his right knee and was in agony every time he bent it; and Hobart was being

*UNITA had warned us that if we escaped we risked being shot by FAPLA forces – who would then lay the blame on UNITA and accuse them of atrocities, such as executing hostages. I am not saying FAPLA would have done this, but it was just a chance we didn't want to take. If I had escaped I would have been very cautious about it. I wouldn't have surrendered to an armed patrol on the road or to a military convoy. I would have made sure I surrendered to a big group rather than to a few individuals. And I would have steered clear of Saurimo, where there were a lot of Russians and Cubans: there could have been political clashes there. Indeed, seeing that there was a military base at Kapenda too, I would probably have made my way slowly back to Cafunfo.

stretchered – as were both the Americans, Al and the Captain.

But Paul wanted to have a go at it. John and I nagged at him not to escape. He had no bushcraft at all and he would have been in a state after a couple of days.

Not that there would have been much practical difficulty in escaping. From the military point of view Major Usabious timed the crossing dead right. It was just dusk when we crossed the road, in five parallel columns, on a moonless night. Once across, we made off into flat, marshy land on its far side. We pushed on, stumbling down the paths through the marshes, till about 11 p.m. Having been told there was no food, we just rolled up in our blankets and went to sleep. Poor fools, we thought this was it for the night.

But about an hour later, about midnight, they woke us up. '*Avanti, avanti. Vam, vam.* Let's go, let's go.' What had happened was that the scouts up ahead had found that a bridge they had built previously had been washed away, and that was why we had an hour's rest: they were rebuilding it. We had to go down this steep, slippery slope and then face this very tricky crossing by underwater bridge. We did it by torchlight, one by one, with one man on one side and one on the other shining their torches on the places where we had to put our hands. It was taking each man – and there were over 300 of us – two or three minutes to cross, on our hands and knees, all getting soaking wet in the process. We came out the other side and then we had to stumble on. This was one of the longest days of effort we went through. We were on the move for eighteen hours in all that day, and a good half of that in total darkness, which demanded the utmost concentration. But on the other hand we knew that we had safely crossed the only asphalt road lying south of Cafunfo, and so by now were well on our way to Jamba. The next major landmarks, many days' march yet to the south, would be first the river Cuango and then the Benguela railway.

There was one other reason, too, why escape for me would have been impractical; and that is that at the moment we crossed the road I was being carried on a stretcher.

Even despite the plastic sandals my feet had started blistering again in several new places, and it had been getting to the stage where it was real agony to put my feet down on the floor at each step. But it was not the plastic sandals that finally laid me out; it was, strangely enough, my new long trousers. As I mentioned earlier, they were small for me, but I had thought that that would sort itself out as I lost weight. It didn't. They were particularly tight under the crutch, and all the time I was walking they were sawing away at me. In the end I was walking bow-legged. I was dropping back: they would keep two men with you and they would stay with you even if you dropped back so far that the whole battalion had passed you by. You would try to catch up and they would start chivvying you to hurry on: '*Vam, vam,* let's go, let's go.' But you just couldn't keep up a fast enough pace to catch up again. So you would stagger into camp two or three hours late, and that would be to your detriment because you would have lost two or three hours' sleep and you might have missed your food. So you did your utmost always to stay with the group.

I was hobbling away, trying to keep up, with these trousers chopping away at me. There was no way of stopping in the original six or seven hours' march, but when we did eventually make a halt, I took these wet trousers off – it was pouring with rain – and put my shorts back on again; though they too were sopping, they were much more comfortable. By then, however, the damage had been done. For the next three or four days we went without washing. The sweat and the muck accumulated around this sore, and it turned septic. I showed the medic my wound – in the crutch – and he put some boracic powder on. That was at about 8 o'clock that night.

About 2 a.m. I awoke, and I was in agony. This stuff had burnt through the skin, and I could peel the skin off in lumps. The whole lot had turned septic. They had to come and shave the hairs off the insides of my legs to try and free everything up. It was just a glued-together mess of infected flesh. I was in such pain that I couldn't even sit up. That was it: I was a stretcher case.

When I tell people now that I spent ten days of the march, on and off, on a stretcher, they smile and imagine that I must have had a pretty cushy time of it, just being carried along for over a hundred miles: a sort of luxury trip through the bush. But in fact it wasn't like that at all. For a start, the two poles running the length of the stretcher were not wide enough apart for my body, so I was tipped to either one side or the other of it, and that caused sores down my hips and my shoulders. My shoulders spread over the poles, and sometimes the bearer, putting his fingers round the poles, would get hold of my flesh and squeeze it, thinking he had hold of a pole. I would curse him for this, and for the vibrations. The bearers would always be trotting along on their heels, out of synch, and the vibrations – up and down, bounce, bounce, bounce – were something unreal.

But what I have to make clear is that they did not carry us as stretcher-bearers in civilized circumstances would, just a foot or two off the ground, with their arms extended. No, they carried us African-style, about six foot up in the air, balanced on their heads. This was much more logical, when you think about it; it spread the weight for them, and meant that they could keep going whereas European-style they would have been totally exhausted within a few minutes over those rough paths. But from our point of view, up on the stretchers high above the heads of the column, it had obvious disadvantages.

There was the question of exposure. Sometimes you would be lying there in the blazing sun, sweating, while your bearers were in the shade; and at other times there would be wind and rain, thunder and lightning up top, and they would be trotting along nice and dry underneath you.

The Captain, who had been on a stretcher longest because of his broken feet, was a bit more devious than the rest of us. He had managed to get himself well organized, with a blanket underneath him, to lie on, a blanket rolled up under his head as a pillow, a tarpaulin that he would pull over him when it was raining, and an umbrella that he would put up when it was hot. But Al had no cap or anything, and he lay face up to the sun all day. He suffered a lot when the sun beat down on him. He was sunburnt and blistered, but by the end of the trip he just looked brown-faced.

Al had this problem with the language. To the Americans I think foreign languages are non-existent. 'Al,' we would say, 'they just don't understand English, particularly your slaughtered English.' We started to try and teach him just a few simple expressions like 'Good morning', '*Bon dia*'. He would go '*bong*' here and '*bong*' there and 'What is that word again?' and we would say '*Bon dia*' and he would say '*Bon geer*'. He just could not fix even this in his mind. If the lads carrying him didn't understand him, he would go about 10 octaves higher and shout. If they still did not understand that, then he would scream.

Many a time it would work. Many a time he would say something to these lads, they would go off and do it, and he would twist round to face us and gloat: 'See? They understand what I say. They are learning.' But not always. On one occasion they had come to a long, rocky slope, and they were trotting downhill, missing these stones, jerking all over the place. Al was waving away from his stretcher, screaming: 'God dammit, will you goddam slow down?' and these blokes were saying in Portuguese, 'Sorry, we can't go any faster, boss', thinking he was urging them on. Many a time my lads would pull off and put me down on the ground for a break, and a moment or two later Al's stretcher would come whizzing past with Al waving and cursing as he disappeared into the distance.

Al had more robust carriers than I did. He had six big-muscled lads. One of mine sounded as if he had TB; his chest would rattle and I would think the lad was dying beneath me. The system was to have a team of six, two carrying the stretcher and the other four trotting behind; when it came to the time for a changeover, the four would lift the stretcher down to the earth and then up you would go again over two different heads. But even with three teams these lads of mine could get so exhausted that they would try to make me walk at places where it was particularly difficult to carry the stretcher. My heels were red raw at the time, and I could walk only on the balls of my feet with a walking-stick. The hardest part was in the morning, actually getting up on to my feet after they were rested. I would need about two or three minutes before I could put all my weight back on to them.

But soon, despite their bad condition, I almost preferred to use my feet rather than to be stretchered; that was because of the real danger with the African system of porterage, which I have not mentioned yet. I saw it first happen to Al. We were tanking along, weaving in and out of the trees, and this vine caught under his chin. His bearers had trotted on probably 15 feet before the vine pulled tight, just hooked him under the chin, and slid him off the stretcher. Al stopped dead, and the stretcher carried on. Crunch! He landed on his back from six feet up. It was hilarious at the time, like a slow-motion cartoon; he could tell exactly what was going to happen, and he screamed to his bearers to halt. But it was inevitable – there was no way he could stop it.

It was less hilarious when something similar happened to

me; though, looking back at it now, that seems comical too. It was daytime in a forest area, there was a clear patch ahead and my bearers picked up speed, aiming at a gap between two trees. But the trees weren't wide enough apart to take the stretcher. The stretcher stopped dead, and hung in the air for a moment as these two prats carried on. Then down we went, pile-driving into the ground, with me flat on my face. The stretcher landed on top of me. They came back, shovelled me on to the stretcher again, dragged me through the gap, then hoisted me up, and off we went as if nothing had happened, merry as could be.

Imagine what it was like, particularly at night, when one of the stretcher-bearers tripped. When the front one tripped, it was reasonably all right because I would land on my feet. But some of them preferred to carry you the other way round, head to tail, and so if the front one tripped and went down I would land on my head. If the back one tripped, which was fortunately rarer, it was even worse. Normally he would shout out, because he was afraid that the stretcher and myself would land on him as he went down. So, at that shout, they would both heave the stretcher to the right and they would run on out of the way while I sailed through the air and landed in a heap on the ground. Nine times out of ten I was lucky and landed on grass or bushes. But once I landed on a tree stump. I thought all my ribs had been caved in. I was in terrible pain, and I had a big blue bruise all over one side of my rib cage for nine or ten days afterwards.

So all the time I was being stretchered, particularly at night, I was in a tense, anxious state, thinking about where they were going to trip next. There was only one time I was really relaxed. I had been on the stretcher about eight or nine hours, without a cigarette or anything. The stretcher-bearers would go on for about three-quarters of an hour at a time, then they would stop for the changeover, and sometimes they would light up and have a smoke among themselves. 'Any chance of a drag off your cigarette?' I asked this particular time.

'All right,' said one of them, passing me the cigarette. I took a big drag off it, and it flattened me. I had never tried it before but I'm sure it was marijuana; and it didn't feel bad at all from then on. I passed the rest of the stretcher trip that day in a pleasant haze.

The last straw came when one of them collided with a tree, the stretcher swung round, and it and myself landed in a jumble across the head of the other bearer, knocking him out cold and ripping the ligaments out of his neck. 'Right,' I said to myself, 'this is it. I don't care if it takes me three months to get to Jamba. I'll walk.'

I could move my legs pretty well by this time, and my feet had healed up too. So I got a walking-stick from the bush, and thereafter I would hobble along, even though many a time I would arrive at camp two or three hours after the rest. The major kept dogging me to go back on the stretcher. 'Please,' he would say, 'please.'

'No, no way,' I would reply. 'No way at all.'

Once we had crossed the asphalt road, tension began to drop and a couple of days later we came to a halt by the side of a big river which, we suspected, marked the beginning of UNITA-held territory. Obviously it was too wide to cross via underwater logs, and there was no sign of a bridge or ford, so we wondered if we were in a quandary here.

But UNITA had an answer for everything. On the trail down we had noticed lots of loot being carried, slung on poles between two men; for instance, it included – we could hardly help noticing this – our two television sets and our video recorders. But there was one mysterious item, also slung between two carriers, and we could not figure out what the hell this might be.

It turned out to be a full-size sea-going dinghy that, blown up, could carry about fourteen people. When we got to the river bank, up these two lads trotted to unpack and assemble it. There was no motor, and that seemed a major snag in view of the strong current. But they fixed a bark rope to the tailgate frame and one of the lads swam across with a load of bark wrapped round him. Then they ferried us, in groups of fourteen or fifteen, back and forth across the river by means of pulling on these bark ropes. They certainly knew how to improvise, the UNITA engineers.

Angola, or at least the interior of Angola away from the coast, the few roads and the one railway, is a very desolate place, and very sparsely populated. In the African countryside in general there is always some sign of human life, but here there was absolutely nothing. It was as it must have been thousands of years ago. All the time we were marching we only saw – and this was the day after our river crossing – one village. There were maybe 2-300 people, including all the women and kids. The villagers were allowed out to watch us pass; we went on another twenty minutes and then halted. A lot of the officers and soldiers then returned to the village to barter for food. Some lads had been carrying new clothes or blankets with them on the way down, and these gradually dwindled away as we went south. As for the radio density, we could see that dropping as we moved down the country. That was how they operated, exchanging loot for food.

We did reasonably well out of it ourselves, considering we had nothing to offer. We were given one quarter of a small banana each, and as that was the first sweet food of any sort we had had for ten days it gave us a real boost. We also did well with tobacco. This village, like others that we bypassed, grew tobacco, and the soldiers would barter for it and plait some for us. We used to get a twisted stub of tobacco about half an inch long whenever they did. The cook boy would issue it to us. Then we would break it up, roll it in a page of paper torn from the exercise book in which we kept the diary, and spit on it as much as we could till it stuck. Sometimes it was like playing a flute.

Four of us were smokers – Paul, John, Al and myself; not the Captain: he probably thought it would damage his health. The Portuguese also smoked and somehow they managed to get about four or five cigarettes a day each, whereas we would have to be content with one. We were fool enough when we had plenty of tobacco at the beginning to give them some; but later on, when the language gave them the advantage for scrounging and we would beg them for a twist of tobacco, no way would they give us any. There were some words said about that.

But we also borrowed a mirror, and that wasn't a boost at all – quite the contrary. The first time we looked at ourselves in this mirror we thought: 'Christ, what a mess!' I have never looked so rag-tag in all my life. We hadn't shaved, and our moustaches were irritating us all the time because our hair was in our mouth. We couldn't close our lips without having to tongue out bits of hair afterwards. We hadn't had a chance to clean our teeth at all, which also felt disgusting. Our beards were itching, and we were continuously scratching away. It was horrible.

It was hilarious, too, in a way. The Filipinos had a shock. All the older ones dyed their hair black, normally; there wasn't a grey-haired one among them when we started. But as they proceeded on the march the dye was growing out and they were turning greyer and greyer. They really started to look their age – which they hated. At this stage Hobart was on a stretcher with breathing problems, Ted had bad feet, and so did Angel: it was age that was knocking him for six. But though those three were stretcher cases and Cookie was in a poor way with the boil on his knee, Roddy, the doctor-surgeon, had given the rest enough confidence in their marching ability to keep going. Francis kept up their morale in the evenings, but he could not do anything to help on the actual march. Roddy could not jolly them through or cheer them up – that was not his way; he could, on the other hand, analyse their mental state for them, and reassure them.

At the beginning there had been a lot of infighting between UNITA and ourselves about Roddy. We had explained when we were captured that Roddy was a fully trained doctor and surgeon, and quite capable of looking after all of us. UNITA refused this. 'We have our own medic and our own medicine for you,' they said. So we did not push the issue. But many times on the march the medic would go and ask Roddy to help him with a patient; and it ended by being the other way round, with their medic acting as assistant to Roddy. Indeed as time went on Roddy was accepted as the unofficial medical adviser to the major, and he would say 'This man needs treatment' or 'That man needs treatment,' suggesting what it should be; mainly he would find himself doing the job too.

The only person who tried to manipulate Roddy was the Captain. He was always manipulating. For instance, he agreed with the cook boy that he would give him his umbrella on arrival at Jamba provided he got all the best bits of meat en route. So it would always be: 'You give me the best bit of meat tonight, or you do not get my umbrella.' It was a mixture of blackmail and bribery, really.

Then he tried it on with Roddy. Roddy came up to me one day and said: 'Boss, I don't know what to do here. The Captain has said that I am to look after him, only him, nobody else. If I look after him, he will set me up in business in America.' To the Filipinos, being set up in business in America is their dream.

'Roddy,' I said, 'if you believe that, you'd believe anything.'

‘That is what I wanted to know,’ said Roddy. ‘Should I trust him or not?’

‘No,’ I said. ‘What’s more, he is being very selfish wanting you to concentrate on him. As far as I’m concerned you don’t look after him any different from anybody else.’

Then I went over to the Captain.

‘Roddy has just told me that you are trying to get him to look after you only,’ I said.

‘That has nothing to do with you,’ he retorted. Then he called me ‘*ein Arschloch*’.

‘*Vielleicht bin ich ein kleines Arschloch*,’ I replied, ‘*aber du bist ein grosses Arschloch*.’*

He was mad that Roddy had told me, and after that he didn’t speak to Roddy for three days.

It had started to rain at 9 o’clock that day, lightly at first, then with the occasional torrential downpour. It continued till 5 p.m., when we had halted for what we thought was the night. We were absolutely soaked through. UNITA made fires – how they did it, I still don’t know – and prepared a meal. But what made us suspicious was that there were no trenches dug or tents put up.

Our suspicions were totally justified. Sure enough, after about three hours, we started off again with the rain absolutely pouring down and we trudged right through the night.

At about 3 a.m. we came to this steep-sided valley. It was still raining, it was absolutely pitch dark, and at the bottom of the valley there was a swamp. That swamp was thick mud, up to the knees, and it was an effort to pick up one foot and plonk it down in front of the other. Paul and John had become separated in the darkness and I was alone with some of the Filipinos. If I had not had the walking-stick to put my weight on I think I might have fallen out even at this stage.

In the middle of the swamp flowed a stream which had been bridged in the usual fashion; but with the torrential rain the water level was two or three feet higher than normal. Crossing that was a nightmare. There were some UNITA lads standing up to their waists in water about 10 feet away, signalling us on, and at first there was a bit of a handrail to cling on to. Then we came to a single trunk, with no handrail or guide, and we were

*‘I may be a small arsehole . . . but you are a big arsehole.’ Somehow it sounds worse in German, but I really meant it.

up to our waists in this current, with a bloke on the bank stretching out his hand to haul us up.

Behind us, suddenly, came a scream and a crash. The handrail had collapsed, and one of the UNITA lads loaded up with ammunition had just vanished. He managed to shed his pack underwater – it was never found – and he surfaced again a bit further down. He swam to the side and waded ashore. So he was all right. But in the darkness and the rain fear easily took a hold.

On the far side of the stream alleyways of bamboo and mangrove trees meandered through the swamp. The mangrove trees had monstrous roots, spreading out in our path, and sometimes – as we were usually wading up to our armpits in water – we had to duck down under the murky water to get past these roots, under and through, clinging to the trunks all the time against the current. At this stage there were just Cookie and myself together, just the two of us, and the only thing that stopped us getting totally lost was the occasional torchlight flash ahead of us through the mangrove trees.

Finally we came to a bit of solid ground, comparatively speaking, where the water was only up to the knees. There were three or four Filipinos on the little patch of higher ground, and one said to me, 'Boss, what about bloody crocodiles?'

That gave me a jolt. I had not thought about this before. Crocodiles were a hazard we simply had not contemplated. But that swamp was just the sort of place you would find crocodiles, lurking there in the dark among the mangrove roots.

'No,' I said, 'crocs don't like fast water. With all this flooding they will be sheltering up somewhere. Don't give it a thought.'

I managed to calm myself down with my own logic. But in actual fact crocodiles will go in fast water, as the Filipinos knew perfectly well. They did not want to go on at all; I had to chivvy them on by going ahead first.

The next stretch was like a horror movie, with the added fear of crocodiles. It was like going through a pitch-black tunnel, with everything grown over, bamboo grasses wrapping themselves viciously around our legs as we tried to grab something stable in order to haul ourselves forward before taking the next step. We were gasping and moaning with the effort, and totally blind. It was raining all the time. The water was up to my armpits, and Cookie, who is shorter than me, was up to his chin. Many a time I could hear him gurgle and blow water out. I kept saying to him: 'O.k., Cookie?'

'Yes, I'm o.k.,' he would gurgle when he could.

We seemed to be changing direction all the time, first across the river, then up river, then down river, then across the river again. Eventually we came out of this nightmarish bamboo tunnel into mangrove forest once more. These were younger trees, not so high, and as we were only waist-deep in water we could lift our legs over them. But the roots were all clumped together, and kept trapping our legs so that we tripped and fell.

Ahead of us some lost UNITA were shouting: 'Which way?' We had no idea. We decided to stay put. We were totally demoralized. The Filipinos behind me were very quiet. Finally, a torch flashed about a hundred yards away and a voice shouted: '*Avanti, avanti!* This way, come.' I let go of the roots I was clinging on to, took a stride in the direction of the light and vanished below the water. I didn't touch bottom and I was grabbing for anything. As I surfaced, my hand seized a root, luckily, and I hauled myself to the side.

'Get back,' I yelled at Cookie. 'Grab hold of something quick; it's very deep.'

What had happened was that I had missed a log bridge that they were trying to signal us on to, and had fallen into the main river current.

By the time that was sorted out, and we were all across on the other side of the river bank, another forty or forty-five minutes had passed and we were all utterly exhausted. The major was there by then, rounding up his strays.

'*Avanti*,' he said. 'Up the hill. Just over the next hill, then we stop on the next ridge.'

I thought to myself: 'I can't even make it to the first ridge, let alone the next one.'

'No,' I said, 'I don't care what you do, you can do as you like, but personally I am not moving.'

Then, ignoring him, I turned to the Filipinos.

'Right, lads,' I said, 'get your blankets and everything and let us find a bit of high ground.'

We moved a little way further up till we found a reasonably level patch with a lot of grass on it. We wrung the blankets out between us – they were soaking wet of course – and we wrapped ourselves in them. It was just cracking dawn, but a late dawn because it was raining – about 5.30 a.m.

We had half an hour's rest before the major reappeared with a new inducement.

'Come,' he said. 'We get to the top of this hill, not the next one, this one, then we light fires.'

He knew how to manage men, that major. He knew when to push, and when to set an example himself, and when to make a concession. He had us up this hill, probably a quarter of a mile, struggling to the top, and somehow UNITA got fires going for us. So then we could dry out our blankets. John and Paul were already there; they and half the battalion had had a far easier time, crossing the swamp by a proper path that the other half, our half, had missed.

All that day we rested up and then at dusk we were on our feet again for the second successive night march. We had expected the journey to get easier, not harder – none of us could understand why we were being pushed so hard at this stage. In fact it was because we were crossing these vast open swamps and plains where there would have been no real cover in daytime against air contact.

That second night it was more plains than swamp; and though this was less sinister, in a way it was worse because we were stumbling along stubbing our feet against tufts of grass at almost every step, and it really hurt. When we fell over these tufts, we would get tangled up in little bushes. On and on it went that way, just on and on, stumble, pain, fall, pain, fall, stumble . . . Sometimes the lad in front of you would start lagging and you could not see far enough in front of him to see if he was still following the man in front. In the end there would be a gap of probably half a mile before we realized that we were on our own, and lost. We would just sit down and wait for UNITA to come back and pick us up. At least it made a break. They would bawl us out, and off we'd go again.

Alternating with the swamps and the plains there were patches of powdery white sand, which was a disaster, particularly in the daytime. When the sun shone – as it did that day – the glare of it gave us splitting headaches. As night fell these eased off, but the sand was hard to walk in. Our feet kept slipping on it, so we used up a lot more energy – of which, by this time, we had very little left.

At 3.30 a.m. we slumped down, exhausted. They let us sleep for three hours, then it was rice and half a corn on the cob for breakfast each, and off we went again. Ahead of us lay our second milestone, so to speak, on our way south: the river Cuango. Compared with what we were used to at Cafunfo, this was a small river, something like 20-25 feet wide, slow-running, very dirty, browny-grey, probably from silt washed down from the hills. We were at its northern bank by lunchtime and had another welcome break there while we crossed by the rubber dinghy, as before. But we were all in poor condition. The only food left now was funge, and we were desperately hungry. Though none of us ever drank stagnant or swamp water, the Captain had bad diarrhoea. Al passed out twice while his feet were being attended to, and the sore in my crutch started turning septic again. The medic gave me an intravenous drip of sugar water, salt and antibiotics but, for all that, the pain became excruciating during the night. Next morning I had to be stretchered again. We had been going for twelve days solid now, and we were coming to the end of our tether. The major tried to keep our morale up by promising us more and better . . . funge!

On the thirteenth day by mid-morning we were passing slit trenches at the side of the path, with patches of tomato and lettuce and corn on the cob growing in the swamps. That gave us a much-needed boost, because we recognized the signs. It meant that we were approaching a base camp; and a base camp would mean the longed-for day of rest. Sure enough, three or four miles further on, there were sounds of singing and dancing, and there was our welcome party come out to meet us. But the celebrations left us indifferent: food, we were thinking, lovely food . . .

'*Hopes are high*,' wrote Paul, whose thoughts, even more than those of the rest of us, seem to have centred on the subject for most of the march, '*for a good meal. These camps are simply a collection of grass huts with pictures of Savimbi stuck up everywhere. There is a unit of UNITA troops here who are well kitted-out and disciplined compared to the 300-odd that have been with us on the march*.'

So much for the setting: then Paul quickly passed on to the important stuff.

'*The mid-day meal was one of the best yet, with a fairly large amount of rice and a little greens and goat meat, but still not sufficient to satisfy us. During the afternoon and evening we rested in the hut built for the five of us*' (that was John, Paul, myself, Al and the Captain), '*which contained spacious grass beds, a real luxury. An entire butchered cow carcass was carried past us and we hope that if we see it again it will be on our plates.*'

That night we slept, cold though it was, like proverbial logs.

Chapter VI

The Long March: 3

Saturday 19 January was the third 'anniversary' of our capture (anniversaries being counted in weeks rather than years), and it was indeed a day of total rest, thank God. Though it was a cold night, we slept on gratefully till way past dawn.

All in all, though, and particularly after our welcome, it was a disappointing day. We never did have a taste of that cow carcass. As John noted in the diary: '*Everyone found breakfast* [rice and some green leaves] *totally inadequate. Lunch consisted of funge. Glen could not eat the funge and had watered down funge and sugar. Funge is similar to wallpaper paste four days old which is brown in colour. Had funge again for dinner.*'

'*The food*,' he rightly summed up, '*is now having a very bad effect on morale*'; and he ended the day's entry rather pathetically with the words: '*Promised a pineapple by the major!*' (Perhaps I was wrong in the previous chapter to imply that Paul was the only one of us whose mind was almost entirely on food!)

Another problem was that this was the day on which they started serious interrogation. As the Captain and Al and Paul quite justifiably explained, 'We were pilots, we never really saw anything,' and as John said, 'I had only been in Angola two weeks before I was captured'; so it all fell to me. They took me off away from the rest and started interrogating me in slaughtered English.

'Your name is Glen Dixon?' they started off.

'Yes.'

'You are the area foreman for Intraco in Cafunfo?'

'Yes.'

Then they wanted to know how many carats the diamond mines at Cafunfo, Dundo and Andrada produced. They wanted to know when we had come back to Cafunfo, on what date we had restarted production, and how long it had continued. There was nothing to hide about this. Production had started up in August and had been halted in September, after the attack on the Luremo mine.

But the major in charge of the interrogation was a nasty piece of work. I didn't like him at all. The trouble was that Ferreira, the Portuguese with whom I had worked in Lucapa, had given him more or less all my past history, including the facts that I had been in the British Army and that I was the man who had opened Cafunfo up again after UNITA's previous attack, in February 1984, had closed it down. They resented that.

'Why did you come back to Cafunfo?' they asked. 'Why were you the first one to come back to Cafunfo?'

The major became really obnoxious at this point and started slagging me off.

'Your character is no good,' he started saying. 'You have no respect for UNITA. You ought to be happy with UNITA because they have rescued you from FAPLA.'

After about half an hour I had had enough of this bullshit and I revved up at him.

'You have done goddam all for me, my friend,' I said: 'You have lost me my job, a good salary and so on. What have I got to be thankful to you for? To me you are just a bunch of hooligans.'

I was really angry. I thought, to hell with it! Anything they have asked us to do we have done, and now I have had enough.

I could see this major would have liked to turn nasty. Had it been up to him he would have had me hanging by the thumbs. But as it was he could only swear at me in Portuguese, which cut no ice with me as I did not understand him.

In English he could not put a sentence together to slag me off properly. I could see him getting frustrated.

'You are a dirty Englishman,' he would say. 'You are a no-good Englishman. Many of you English are hypocrites.' And so on and so forth. It didn't make any odds to me, as he was probably right.

Then they started asking me about the troops. It was a bit ironic in a way because there was the good guy, the soft guy, the guy that was there to butter you up, as well as the nasty. How many troops were there in Andrada? How many here, how many there?

'I cannot tell you how many troops there are in Andrada,' I replied. 'I am not a military man, I am here as a civilian working for a civilian government.'

'It is not a civilian government. It is a Marxist government.'

'It is still a civilian government to me,' I said. 'I am not here to be for the government or against it.'

Then they asked: how many troops were there in Cafunfo?

'You should know better than me,' I said. 'You attacked the place. Your surveillance had got to be better than mine.'

But as they went on and on repeating the question, and I didn't want to make trouble for myself unnecessarily, I ended by saying that I thought there were about 300. There was no point in lying.

'How many Cubans are there in Dundo?' they asked next. 'How many Russians are there in Dundo? Why will you not tell us?'

'I will be honest with you,' I replied. 'I don't know. I know there are some there. But how many I have no idea.'

Next they wanted to know about heavy machine-gun emplacements.

'You are talking about things I don't know about,' I said.

Then it was the air base at Saurimo.

'How many planes are at Saurimo?'

'I don't know.'

'Have you seen aeroplanes at Saurimo?'

'Yes.'

'What aeroplanes have you seen?'

'Ilyushin transport planes, MIGs, P8s.'

'How many?'

'I have no idea.'

This went on and on, with them repeating the same questions over and over again. It got really monotonous. And it put me in no mood for the two-hour rally laid on for us, as usual, that day, with the words UNITA and Savimbi being forever repeated in every song or speech or chant. The interrogation had really turned me off UNITA and everything to do with it, including its president.

The major even came to wake me up that night, and the next night too – trying to catch me off-balance, I suppose. He came by at 2 a.m., and later, with more questions.

'I just wanted to make a point,' he would say, trying to prod. There was only him and me awake. I would leave him sitting there like a fool while I would take maybe five minutes to answer his question.

'Why don't you answer me?'

'I am waking up,' I would reply. 'I am trying to think.'

Even when we started off marching again next morning he continued to nag at me, to pester me. We started off in better spirits, though, because *our* major kept his word about the pineapple – we had two square inches each for breakfast – and Captain Cat told us that we were only ten days away from Jamba (though knowing how reliable he wasn't, we did not take that too seriously). But what we always took seriously was food. In the morning UNITA caught a small buck; and in the evening we were brought a bit of meat with gravy. We found it was rump steak. It was beautiful, absolutely fantastic.

Meanwhile this pillock, the interrogating major, had been trying to keep up his questions and to irritate me. I always liked to keep about two yards between myself and the man in front; it meant I did not have to bend my head so far down to watch the track. He would keep silent, saying nothing to anybody, then he would sneak up on me.

'Englishman, why don't you walk quicker?'

'I am effing fed up of walking quicker,' I told him.

'What does this "effing" mean?' he asked.

'Up yours,' I replied.

He tried to figure out something to come back at me again, but he could not find the words in English, so off he would go, pissed off.

When we stopped for a meal and a rest at mid-day, he waited till I had dozed off, and then he woke me and started on the questions again. That night it was the same thing. But John was snoring his head off, and Paul was snoring, so he couldn't get anywhere. Next day, fortunately for me, we lost him. However, another interrogation officer took his place. This one was a captain, and though he was a bit like the Sergeant Major in the film *The Wild Geese* – pretty abrupt and tough – he tried handling it the friendly way. But that was almost worse, because he used to spend hours and hours rephrasing the same series of questions. I was totally fed up with this talking. It was all pointless. But our impression was that each of these interrogation officers was trying to make a name for himself as the expert in getting information out of prisoners. In actual fact they got no information except what they must have known already. All they succeeded in doing – I hope Jonas Savimbi will note this if he ever reads this book – was putting our backs up.

(We thought that when we arrived in Jamba the interrogations would be much harder, if the present interrogations were anything to go by. We were worried in case we let anything slip, as all our workmates were still up north. Yet when we arrived in Jamba, there was not one question about anything. We were baffled.)

By now they were pressing us less hard – the average day's march was 12 miles, not 18 as before – and we were beginning to take more of an interest in life in general. We managed to scrounge a pair of scissors and tidy up the long hairs on our moustaches, which was a relief. Paul and John played 'battleships' that afternoon, after the day's march, while Al and I made a draughts board. Al had a combination knife with a little saw on it. So we got a stick about one inch in diameter and sawed off round sections. Half of these discs we put a cross on: those were the black, and the other half, unmarked, were the white. Then, on a piece of the exercise book, we drew the squares in biro, and there was our draughts board.

The only thing that had caused confusion was, as usual, Al's variants of the English language. He insisted on talking about 'checkers' when he had the idea, and I could not make out at first what he was on about.

Another time he had said: 'I would love some of those crunchies.'

Immediately our minds flicked back to chocolate honeycomb Crunchie bars in England.

'Why are you going on about Crunchies?' we said. 'You can't get Crunchies here, you nerd.'

'No,' said Al, 'you got me wrong. I mean those yellow things with knobs on.'

'What are you talking about?'

'The things we had the other day.'

'Oh, *mealies!*' said John, using the South African term for corn on the cob. It was bad enough John half talking South African English without Al's slaughtered American English as well.

We were getting really ingenious about improvising by this time. When we were in the bush marching we had used for toilet purposes a particular broad leaf, shiny on one side but with a velvet surface on the other. It made beautiful toilet paper. So whenever we came into an area of these broad-leaf plants we would grab handfuls. But in the base camps there was nothing. However, in the last base camp there were hundreds of little posters, about 7 inches long and 5 inches wide, with the UNITA flag on one side and the portrait of President Savimbi on the other. So we used those. But somebody must have peered down into the hold and seen this load of UNITA flags lying at the bottom of the loo. There was a big rumpus. We were lined up and told that to use these flags for improper purposes was a punishable offence, and in future anyone found doing so would be jailed indefinitely once we reached Jamba. So we went back to the leaves.

There were also larger posters at the base camp, with quite a bit of slagging off on them: '*Foreigners Are Hypocrites*', '*Foreigners Must Leave Angola*' – that sort of thing. Paul nipped out in the night and nicked one of these. They would have given him a severe dogging if they had caught him; and they might even have strung him up as an example if they had found out what he was planning to use it for.

We used it for loo paper and Paul also made a tobacco pouch out of it, which was very useful to all of us too. By this time we were in totally unpopulated, heavily wooded areas, weaving in and out of trees, with the engineering platoon up front sometimes having to hack its way through elephant grass eight or nine feet high. There were no villages or signs of cultivation for mile upon mile. So we had to rely on wild tobacco. The cook boy would hand it out to us whenever he had a share. It was green, of course, and the system was to lay the leaves out on top of our blankets and tie them on so that they would dry in the sun. When I say 'leaves', we would probably get one leaf a day, which would make four cigarettes. So Paul carried all our dry leaves in this tobacco pouch; and John would roll the cigarettes, because John was the person who could roll the thinnest cigarettes.

The next problem was getting a light. We had had these Zippo lighters originally, but of course with one lighter for fifty or sixty people, it was flick, flick, flick all the time; and within a week the flint had gone or the lighter fuel had run out. So what the UNITA lads did to get a light was, in effect, to adapt stone-age techniques.

They would take a piece of hardwood with a hollow indentation in it and a piece of softwood with a kind of bow attached. Then they would break open a bullet, pour the gunpowder into the hollow in the hardwood base, fix a little bit of dry moss round the edges, then just whang the bow a couple of times, twirling the softwood stick around – and puff! they had a light. Of course they lost the bullet. At a rough estimate, between Cafunfo and Jamba they must have expended 3,000 rounds in lighting up cigarettes.

'*Twenty-five days in the bush now,*' noted Paul in the diary, '*and life is a little easier as we become accustomed to it. But none of us is getting any stronger. John is suffering badly with foot pains, although he has no visible symptoms.** *Al is being stretchered and dropped occasionally but Glen is trying to walk so as to avoid the stretcher hazards. The Captain is walking all the time now but still suffers from stomach problems. I feel reasonably fit, much better than two days ago. But we are told we will be walking tonight, which we dread, as night marches are the worst experience so far.*'

In fact, however, that night march was not as bad as the previous ones – except for John, who had to be helped along at the end. He had had a pair of good work boots on, but, having burnt his socks, he had problems with the balls of his feet, and the arches. He suffered a lot, and was in agony sometimes, but he always managed to keep walking.

As for the Captain, he had spent most of his time so far on the stretcher. When he got fed up, he'd tell his bearers to put him down and he would have a hobble along. Though he never suffered from blisters, he was always in pain with his broken feet – which we did not properly realize or give him credit for at the time. We thought he was blathering a bit, especially since on occasion, as on this night march, he showed he could walk. But that was his personal form of courage and proving himself, really.

Everyone crashed out as soon as we halted, two hours before dawn, and we had an easy time of it for the rest of the day. Though it rained very heavily we managed to stay dry under our tarpaulins. We even had a small piece of banana each, to add flavour to the funge.

But what certainly made that day different from all the others was that a new battalion arrived to take over as our escort for the rest of the march. Our old battalion, having come so far, was due to return to the Cafunfo area – I suppose because it was the more experienced, though it seemed hardly

*He had burnt his socks, the pillock, not having learnt from Al's experience; that was why.

fair on the men, seeing that they were certainly in need of a rest and a bit of refitting.

'*Bad start to the day*,' noted Paul in the next diary entry. '*We are woken at 2.05 a.m. by Lieutenant "Gob" – his final duty with us and we will not really miss him.*'

Gob had been giving us stick all the way down, every day trying to push us a little bit more. But we did miss the other officers, Captain Cat, Major Usabious and the other major, not least because no one in this new unit could speak English, so we had virtually no means of communication.

Before dawn we passed through a Portuguese village on the crest of a hill. It was an eerie experience. There were brick buildings with Portuguese tiles on, telephone cables, electric pylons – it looked as if it must have been a really nice place to live in. But it was totally deserted; there was not a single soul living there. It must have been an agricultural settlement for Portuguese colonists coming out from the poorer parts of Portugal to farm, and I imagine they had packed it in at Independence, ten years earlier.

As we left this Portuguese village, we had to go down a long old road, across an old wooden bridge, and then up a steep hill. It was the coldest dawn yet. I was feeling o.k. but weak. We took a few minutes out on the crest, to have a cigarette, but we couldn't find a light. '*Vam, vam*,' they said. I stood up – and immediately fell over. I had no sense of balance at all. I was on my hands and knees, with the officers gathering round asking me what the matter was. I tried to stand up again, but over I went, hitting this captain on the thigh as I went down. I just could not get back up again. So they helped me to my feet, and supported me for a minute or two. Once we started walking, I said, 'O.k. that's o.k.'; and I went on for about another hour and a half, though things were a bit blurred in front of me. I knew I had a problem but I could not figure out what it was. Then round a corner – it was light now, about 8 o'clock – we came upon an archway decorated with UNITA flags and marched into the battalion's temporary base camp, our destination for the day. There were no huts or grass shelters but there were beds, out in the open, through the woods. I sat down on one and keeled over backwards.

I don't remember much after that. When I came to, I found a medic rubbing my arm with antiseptic and pushing a needle in. They attached me to an intravenous drip carrying a white liquid: dextrose. I went to sleep. When I woke, the first thing I saw was a strange woman, quite a handsome woman, with a big bowl on her head which she lowered. Inside this bowl were brown objects. I looked back up, and I saw John and Paul sitting nearby watching me, laughing and carrying on.

'What is that over there then, Paul?' I asked.

'Bloody biscuits with peanut butter on,' he said, savouring each word.

Normally I hate peanut butter, but on this occasion I staggered to my feet, went across to this woman, and she gave me two biscuit sandwiches with peanut butter dripping from in between – and it was thick.

It wasn't till I had these two biscuits in my hand that I realized that I was still attached to the dextrose drip. I had been dragging it along the ground, and the blood had started running back down the tube. So I had to hold the peanut-butter concoctions in one hand, careful not to squash them for fear of losing a single drop, and with the other pick up the dextrose drip, take it back and stick it on its pole again. The medic found me happily sitting there squeezing these biscuits and licking the peanut butter out, and he proceeded to drain the drip, clean it, and re-attach it. They put two pints into me, and what with that and the vitamins I felt great. It really gave me a lot of power.

In fact things improved immensely once we had reached this camp. Our new escort battalion had established it as its base about 12 miles short of its rendezvous with us the day before; it had dropped off most of its supplies and troops there, sending out just the officers with a company escort to bring us in. The battalion had come up from Jamba and had brought plenty of supplies with it, including high-protein raspberry, caramel and chocolate bars. We would eat one of these bars over a period of, say, an hour, and would feel the energy flowing back into us. I have never felt food do anything like that to me before. It was unreal. We were also given orange juice, which was marvellous at first – though later it fermented, and that was deadly. And that night we had an improved type of funge, about 30 per cent corn, which was served with a little bit of boiled pork and gravy. Morale shot up.

Al and Paul had been feeling weak, too. They were given penicillin shots, almost at once, and their condition improved. As for the Captain, he looked after himself as usual. He came up behind the girl issuing these high-protein bars, and as she was lifting them out of her cardboard box he plunged his hands in, grabbed two enormous handfuls and stuffed them into his shirt. Two days later, when there were no more at all available for the rest of us, the Captain was still nibbling away at these bars day and night. He must have nicked something like 25 of them. We were disgusted.

Next morning, though, before the scarcity, they melted down some of this caramel and gave us a hot caramel drink, plus peanut-butter biscuits again, to start us off – the best breakfast we had had so far. So, though it was 2.30 a.m., we set off in high spirits; and that day we had a beautiful day's march. Some of the scenery was absolutely fantastic. There was steep climbing that day, but both Al and I were walking well, and we would come out of the high wooded areas and look out over a winding valley with outcrops of rock all reflecting different colours: purple, red, blue and green.

One open area we marched through was just rolling hills covered in marigold and wild roses. The streams in between were crystal clear. One especially sticks in my memory, falling down eight feet in about forty tiers, like a tiny, carefully engineered waterfall in red rock, with wild flowers at its edge and the sun hitting it at exactly the right angle, giving the falls a beautiful pink glow.

We walked all morning. Then, after an excellent lunch of corned beef mash with gravy and orange juice, we did a four-hour stint in the afternoon that led us to another camp where individual grass huts had already been prepared. And there we had our best night's sleep yet. We were not woken this time till 7 a.m., and then with the sun shining.

I have to say that if we had had twice as long to do that march, and if we had been properly kitted out and prepared – well, it is the sort of trekking holiday that people from Europe or America might have paid £1000 each to go on. We were waited on hand and foot all the way, we had our meals cooked, our laundry done, our camps laid out for us; we didn't have to lift a finger for ourselves – only our feet. 'My men had a hard time bringing you down from Cafunfo,' Jonas Savimbi was to say to us later. 'They went to a lot of trouble with you,' and there was no way we could fail to agree with him.

To add to our pleasure, the next day, Saturday 26 January, our fourth 'anniversary', was, despite some confusion – some starting and stopping – a day of total rest; and lunch was so copious – corn funge, beans with a little corned beef in gravy – that, after eating about 4 lbs of this each, both John and Paul for the first time since leaving Cafunfo had to give up and leave something on their plates. Furthermore we were now told that the transport – lorries that would take us the final leg to Jamba – lay only a few days' march ahead, on the other side of the Benguela railway. So everyone was cock-a-hoop at the thought of the end of our long march being in sight.

Everyone, that is to say, bar myself. I remembered having read a newspaper account by a lad who had been captured previously, Neil Hare; he had said that the trip in the vehicle was worse than the walking. As we were being pushed on hard over the next four days, I would say to the others: 'You might be grumbling now about the walking, but when you get in that truck, you will regret this.'

'No,' they would reply, 'I don't care what you say. The truck has got to be better than what we are going through now.'

There was one other point niggling away at me, and that was the whereabouts of our money and documents that the battalion which had captured us had been 'looking after' on the march down.

'You did manage to get these from the last battalion?' I asked.

'This is UNITA,' they assured me. 'It is all organized, we are not *bandidos*.'

However, events were ~~to~~ prove that I was only too right – unfortunately – to be worried about both these problems.

The first day of this final stretch was fine; but by the second day the improved food had run out, cigarettes had run out, the pace was being pushed, the weather had turned hot and humid, and we were being tormented by a new plague, the *nipani* fly.

Nipani flies are very small flies with no brains whatsoever. They are attracted by sweat; when the sun shines and it is hot, they are at their worst. I have been stung by scorpions and they don't bother me, but flies – I have a thing about flies. I hate them. These *nipani* flies were really irritating. Two or three hundred of them would be dancing around our heads, flying into our eyes, our mouths, up our nostrils, into our ears. Our hair would be wet with sweat, and they would be landing on our hair, where we could feel them struggling. Everybody was covered in these flies now that we were at a lower altitude, though the UNITA officers had something like a fishing net that they dropped down over their shoulders. (The ordinary UNITA lads just seemed able to ignore the flies.) But they simply tormented us. In the daytime we couldn't sleep or rest because they would swarm over us. At the end of the day our hands would be covered in the purple-ish blood of these flies where we had been swiping them and crushing them. But as soon as it got cool or the shadows came, they were gone and it was beautiful.

On the second day out we crossed a vast, open plain. For some reason we did not go across at the narrowest point as before, we went down its total length. It must have been a 12- or 15-mile stretch, and it was hard marching. It was flat, luckily, like a white chalk plain with very fine grass over the chalk. In a way it was like Wiltshire. But the trouble was that it was one of those African plains where there are knobs of grass all over the place. Sometimes you couldn't put a foot down without hitting one. So your feet were at different angles, and it was a head-down job all the way across. You could see the blue haze of the trees in the distance, and you would keep your head down for maybe an hour, watching where you were walking. Then you would look up, hoping it was a bit closer, but the distance just did not seem to change.

This went on for hours and hours. At first UNITA set a very fast pace. But in the end I took over as pacemaker and I kept a steady pace. I was yelled at and abused and pushed to go faster, but I wouldn't. When I had had enough of this, I would just stop; and everyone else would come to a halt too, behind me.

'O.k.,' I would say, 'what's your problem?'

'You are not going fast enough.'

'Why must I go faster?' I would ask.

'You must walk faster,' said the major, 'because our leader is waiting for you in Jamba.'

'If we go faster,' I would reply, 'then we start having fall-outs, people dropping out. Let us stay at a steady pace all day.'

They could not see the sense of that at all. But I stayed as pacemaker and went on doing it my way, despite these set-tos. If Filipinos had been in front and the UNITA lads had shouted at *them* to go faster, they would have done so; and the lads struggling at the back would of course have been left behind.

By this time I was a bit of an odd shape. I was losing a lot of weight because of lack of food and the extreme pressure we were under. My legs were really muscly; they had lost fat off the top and after a few hours' walking the muscles were corded really tight. But the top half of my body had been doing nothing, and it had just wilted away. 'Jesus,' said John, walking behind me, 'you ought to see your legs!' We were all the same, of course, but it was particularly noticeable on me because I was wearing short trousers.

But however powerful our leg muscles were by then, it was a real endurance test crossing those plains because of the conditions underfoot, the heat and the *nipani* flies, and the thirst. We were nine hours without a drop of water or anything. But it is surprising how we had learnt by now to control our thirst. The trick was to keep swallowing saliva; if you stopped doing this, your throat would become dry and it would be hard to swallow. Another trick was to march with the mouth closed, which is hard (and impossible if there is an uphill stretch), because if you breathe through the mouth you lose a lot of water vapour. When this happens, you feel the hot air coming in and drying out your throat, and it gets really sore and painful.

But good fortune saved us from the worst effects. After hours of marching in single file we noticed the scouts up ahead bending down and picking things up off the ground. 'Hello,' we thought, 'what's this?' Then gradually half the battalion which was ahead of us – that is, 150 men – was spreading out over a width of about 60 or 70 yards and doing the same.

'Right, lads,' I said, 'spread out and let's look for whatever it is these cretins are picking up.'

It turned out to be a round fruit that they called *kabungo*, yellowy orange in colour, about an inch to an inch-and-a-quarter in diameter. When we broke these fruits open, they were something like a chestnut, divided into three or four sections, each with skin, flesh and a kernel inside. We put these in our mouths and sucked. They were very sweet and quite juicy: I had never tasted anything like it, a beautiful taste.

While we were picking these *kabungos* up, shoving them in our shirts and so on, we were off the track. The major kept bawling us out, because we were spread all over the savannah, and trying to push us back into line. But we just wouldn't have it. It may seem amazing that we were able to disobey men with guns in their hands when we were their prisoners. But by this time we reckoned we knew how far we could push it with them, and we knew they would never treat us brutally. Even Lieutenant Gob, a pushy 19-year-old and the trickiest of the lot, at his worst would only manhandle us, shove us around a bit; he would never wave his revolver or threaten physical violence. So for the whole of that last stretch, maybe over six miles, we were straggling all over the place as we pleased, collecting these fruits.*

The major's worries, however, had not been as pernickety as they seemed at the time. We were approaching the Benguela railway, which runs right across the country from Zaire in the east down to the port of Benguela on the west, on the Atlantic ocean; this railway, which divides the country into two, north and south, is the strategic objective in the continuing Angolan civil war. The very next afternoon, at about 4 o'clock, we were just beginning to move down into a very big valley when we heard a drone in the distance. As the sound came closer it was unmistakable – FAPLA helicopters. We stopped on the edge of the treeline. In the distance we could see these two big helicopter gunships moving across – flying high, admittedly (you could not have shot them down with a rifle), but coming directly towards us.

'Cover up all your yellow slickers and bright colours and get under the trees,' I yelled at the Filipinos.

The UNITA lads were just laughing at us.

'Take no notice of them. Just get under the trees,' I said.

It took the helicopters ten minutes to come up to us; when they were directly overhead, the lads who had been doing the laughing moved, a bit sheepishly, under the trees themselves. It was an anxious moment. If we had been out in the open and moving, we would certainly have been spotted and strafed.

We sat still for another ten minutes till the gunships had disappeared into the distance. Then we crossed this open valley into the wooded area on the other side.

Bugger me if the helicopters didn't come back again. We sat it out under cover, thanking our good luck that they had not

*Apart from using wild tobacco leaves, this was about the only time we lived off the land, except for one other occasion when we found some purple fruit, white inside. Though this had a very bitter taste, it would quench our thirst and we were scoffing it all day, chuffed, because this was vitamin C and that was what we needed. But that night we had stomach-ache, diarrhoea, and so on.

caught us in the valley; and as soon as they had passed directly overhead, we were up and marching through the bush again. It seemed a bit too soon to me. But UNITA weren't worried.

'It is 5 o'clock,' the major said. 'They are knocking off. They are going home.' And he was proved right, as it happened.

It was a long, long drag up to the railway, an hour and a half's climb – hard-going. We crossed it at 6.30 p.m., exactly one calendar month after we had been captured. When we got to the railway itself, there was a short, steep embankment, then a stone wall.

It was a single-line railway. There was a white post with two markers on: 879/11 – possibly a distance mark in kilometres and a level drop in metres.

'As you cross,' said the major, 'step on the sleeper. Do not step on the stones in between.'

There were two soldiers standing on sleepers, and the middle sleeper was the one he signalled us on to.

'Why?' we asked.

'It is possible that FAPLA have laid landmines,' he explained, 'because this is one of our crossing points.'

Apparently UNITA have something like thirty regular crossing points over the railway, and the tracks are pretty well-worn. The railway itself, they told us, had been disused for six or seven years. But in this respect I did not believe them. Had this been the case, the tops of the rails would have been thoroughly rusted over. However, there were still faint scratch marks visible, and I would say that a train, no doubt heavily escorted, had passed over within the last month or so. However that may be, the actual crossing of the railway put us decidedly in the southern half of the country and gave us a real sense of achievement and satisfaction. Also we knew that the transport was very near now. That night, after crossing the railway, we went on for only another two hours before reaching a camp. The end of our long march was looming. Four hours to the transport, we were told.

But our hopes were raised only to be disappointed. This particular UNITA battalion was much less expert at finding its way than our original battalion. They had no one of the calibre of Major Usabious as pathfinder, and they were continually going astray and getting lost. We were by now rapidly coming into the low country, where, for the first time, mosquitoes were beginning to be a problem. We must have dropped down 1500 feet after crossing the Benguela railway. On the march we had been issued with one malaria tablet about every ten days, but by now UNITA had run out of malaria tablets and they were giving us quinine powder mixed up with water. It was vicious stuff. They would sit down and watch us drink half a pint of this muck, all brackish and discoloured.

In one way it did the job. None of the English went down with malaria. But probably because of the water both John and myself went down with chronic diarrhoea. 'The transport is one hour more,' the major kept saying. But it never was. We had been crossing a swampy area in the morning, then in the afternoon there was very dense bush, with big trees, uphill and down dale; the contours of the land were very sharp, with no streams, so drinking water was difficult to obtain.

'*We were near exhaustion*,' wrote Paul in the diary. '*Morale falling as our health declines and despite promises made by UNITA the transport fails to appear. We requested that we should make camp and to our relief this was agreed upon.*'

All that night I lay awake suffering from diarrhoea. Reveille came at 5 a.m., and we were off an hour later – promised, once again, that the transport was very close. This time, however – no doubt to avoid a real fiasco, going straight past the transport – UNITA abandoned the single-file system. They split into five or six columns and spread out into a line that may have extended over as much as three-and-a-half miles, with ourselves roughly in the middle. So we were covering a wide area as we started marching. We all moved through the bush in line; and a couple of hours later, all of a sudden, we came on to this newly-beaten track, a vehicle track. And there, standing on it, was this battered old Mercedes lorry.

You could have heard our cheers for miles.

Chapter VII

In the Lorry

We were five days in the lorry, and in those five days we must have covered about 600 miles – I would say about the same as we had done in over a month of marching. It is well nigh impossible to be exact about distances in Angola, and even published maps of the country seem to disagree with each other, but although the distance from Cafunfo to Jamba can be measured as about 600 miles and we can plot our route in general terms, we have no way of working out precisely where all the false trails and deviations to avoid FAPLA (as I mentioned earlier, we started by making for the Zaire border), the doublings back, retracings of steps when we lost our way, and circuits round obstacles took us. All we know is that we must have covered about twice the distance between start and finish that any proverbial crow would have done. The lorry, too, followed a far from direct route down to Jamba, over the roughest of ground.

Riding in the lorry was not enjoyable – not at all. For the first half hour it was great to be on the road eating up the miles. An hour later it was still better than walking. After another hour there was not that much difference, as regards discomfort, between walking and being on the vehicle. Then, after that, it was just downright misery.

This was partly because the journey had got off to a bad start, with the usual UNITA muddle we had come to associate with this escort. We had hardly been loaded into the Mercedes – which needed a bump start to get it going – before we were all unloaded again and switched to a Russian truck which had passed us going the other way. We were all jammed into the Mercedes like sardines, about 23 of us and about 20-22 UNITA, including the cook girls and all their pots and pans. There had been a punch-up as everyone tried to sit down and get comfortable. On first sight of the Russian vehicle we had hoped that there would now be two lorries for us, and we could spread ourselves, have a bit of space. Some hope! We were ordered out of the one, moaning and groaning, and into the other, all fighting and squabbling for room.

The whole operation must have taken over an hour.

The Russian vehicle was facing the way we had just come. On the front of this vehicle was a massive steel bumper, so the driver put his left hand hard down, bulldozed his way through the bush, then back on to the road and away we went. I say 'road', but in fact there were simply tracks – two grooves in the ground weaving in and out of the trees. Many a time elephants had pushed trees down across the tracks and we had to blast our way through. Also, tree roots were growing up even between the tracks, and often the vehicle would bounce out of the tracks – particularly at night – and ricochet off into the bush. As luck would have it, we never hit any really big trees, though that night at one point as we were going down a hill the driver went off the road. It was pitch black, he was going like the clappers and he only had one headlight working. As we ploughed through the bush, he stood on everything he had to try and stop; finally we screeched to a halt about four feet away from an enormous tree standing directly in our path. If we had hit it it would have split the truck in two or crumpled it up. Night-driving was really nerve-wracking.

And, night or day, it was bone-wracking too. We were packed so tight, with people sitting on each other's feet and crushed up against each other's arms, that whenever we hit a bump everyone and everything left the floor together and then came back down with a crash and a long-drawn-out groan of 'ooooh!' It was agony.

It was cold in the back of that steel-bodied truck when the sun went down, and we huddled against each other for warmth. The Captain was jammed up against me.

'Let us sing some old German songs, military songs,' he said.

I knew he had been a Hitler Youth till he was 15 or 16; then, when the war ended, he had knocked around Germany till he had won a scholarship to go to university in America, and there he had met his wife, who like him was Austrian.

'O.k.,' I said.

So he started singing a few of the well-known German military songs, and I joined in where I could. Then he said: 'What about the Hitler Youth anthem and the Horst Wessel Lied?'

'I don't know any of the Nazi war songs,' I replied.

But he was totally unabashed. He started singing, and he

went through every regiment in the German Army and every regimental song. He had a good memory, you have to give him that. But after about two hours of this I said: 'I have had enough. You either shut your rattle or sing something else.'

'I thought you knew them,' he said, indignantly. 'You worked with the German people for ten years.'

That totally lost me.

'I did,' I said. 'But that has nothing to do with being a bloody Nazi. You are an Austrian, not a German, and pro-Nazi because you are an Austrian, I can understand that. But myself I am anti-Nazi, so I am not interested.'

'You know that most German people are pro-Nazi,' he said.

'You are wrong, mate. Some, maybe,' I replied. 'But it's the Austrians we're talking about.'

Having worked with many Austrians, I know that quite a few of the older ones are pro-Nazi; he was certainly one of them. Yet I would not go as far as to say that he was a Nazi himself. I don't think he was inclined to feel that he was racially superior; indeed, he often astounded and annoyed us because, on the contrary, he was so subservient. When he came up against any authority, even if it was just a corporal, it was 'Yes, sir. No, sir.' It was always 'Sir,' 'Sir,' 'Sir'. It was embarrassing. He gave us the impression of being very timid and totally lost, totally out of his environment. If they brought him food, for example, he would go over the top: '*Muinto bem*, *muinto bem*, excellent, very good, the best food I have had for years.' All this sort of crap came pouring out, and it really got on our nerves. Even the UNITA lads would shrug and roll their eyeballs upwards, as if to say, 'What a pillock this man is!' He really was most peculiar.

He was also a most selfish man; he had no sense of humour or fair play at all, as an incident that occurred that night and that was totally unforgettable went to show.

It was past midnight, dry but bitter cold, when we drove through a big archway and into a complex that was much more elaborate than any base camp we had seen as yet. There were water towers, fuel pumps, a workshop and various other facilities. We got off the vehicle, bone-sore and chilled through, pulled our blankets around us and staggered around a bit, not knowing the form, till we were gathered up and led off by a UNITA officer. He took us to a big hut; inside, the first thing that struck us was that there was a 40-watt electric light bulb hanging from the ceiling - the first electric light we'd seen for nearly five weeks.

The scene it illuminated was even more striking. Right round the room there were bamboo bench seats with backs on, built into the walls. There were tables in front of them with - of all things! - tablecloths on them. 'Jesus,' we thought, 'what is this?' We were told to come and sit down. Then a bevy of UNITA cook girls appeared bringing in big dishes of potatoes – which we had not seen since we were captured – and corned beef. We were told we could have as much as we liked, so we really gorged ourselves. It was paradise.

Five minutes later three more girls came in bringing in big three-gallon chrome thermoses with something steaming out of the spout. Another girl distributed tin mugs to each one of us, and began to pour. We could hardly believe our eyes – or our noses. It was thick black coffee. It was absolutely delicious.

A big bowl of sugar appeared, and we could help ourselves to as much as we liked. Then another girl came in and apologized to all of us because there was only one tin of condensed milk. She punched two holes in it and handed it to the Captain because, I imagine, he looked like the most senior white man present.

The Captain, without hesitation, emptied over half of the condensed milk into his own tin mug till the coffee was running over the top. I could hardly believe it, even though it was happening before my very eyes.

'What about the rest of us?' I finally choked out.

'That's your problem,' he said calmly.

I sandblasted him in German.

'Captain,' I said, 'if I had the energy I would take you outside and I would beat seven bells out of you, I really would. *Du bist ein Schweinhund!*'

It did not bother him at all, that was the extraordinary thing. He could not see that he had done anything wrong. The next morning he came up to me and said, 'Morning, Glen' as if nothing had happened.

It takes the Filipinos time to weigh people up – quite a bit of time, actually. But on the next occasion the Captain came round to join our group – me, Al and the two other British lads – we all got up and moved ten feet away. He went over to the Filipinos, and even they did the same. Every group moved away from him. We were all totally and utterly sick of him. But even this did not seem to bother him. As I have said before, he was a most peculiar man.

Because he was a keep-fit freak, though, he always chewed his food carefully – when we were given biscuits, he would sit like a rabbit and chew; one biscuit would probably take him twenty minutes to absorb into his stomach. And on this particular occasion that certainly saved him. Because, though Al and I were moderates at the best of times, John and Paul had really gorged themselves. Next morning John vomited when we were woken up, and he looked bad. There was a bit of an argument, even though – for the first time – we were sleeping in separate cubicles, so I was not huddled up against him when he vomited.

'Bloody serves you right for pigging yourself last night,' I said. 'I told you not to pig yourself.'

John had hit one of his low points over the previous couple of days; he had been very quiet, saying even less than usual, and he was obviously feeling in a poor way. Paul, on the other hand, would just chatter on about nothing; the only thing to do with Paul was to ignore him and let him get on with it. But on this particular occasion Paul backed John up. There was not exactly a quarrel, but certainly a bit of animosity between the three of us – almost for the first and last time. However, it only lasted a few minutes.

About 11 a.m. we started wondering why we were sitting there all day when we were still two or three days' drive from Jamba. We were informed that the truck was being serviced. That was good news for John in his condition, and indeed it proved good news for all of us because the medic came round and attended to our feet.

He spent about an hour on mine alone. What we had developed were lots of white patches. We had not paid much attention to these, though they were tender, because much more serious things had seemed to be wrong with our feet. The medic explained that these white patches were each caused by a piece of sand that had been ground into our skin and that the skin had grown over. He proceeded to lance these white patches and squeeze them, and sure enough inside each was a little grain of sand. Around this, the whole area had turned septic. This white septic stuff was hard, and it took some squeezing out. But our feet certainly felt much better after he had done this. For the first time in weeks we found that we could actually walk without wincing.

We were woken at 3 a.m. on the morning of 2 February; and after a delayed start that had even us shouting impatiently '*Avanti! Avanti!*' off we went. It was continuous driving from then onwards.

As Paul wrote in the diary entry for the following day: '*We recall this period as three days and three nights of constant misery, and it is impossible now to distinguish one day from another with certainty. Although there is no way that we would have preferred to walk the distance covered by the truck this experience, along with the night marches, is the worst of our lives.*'

What made life in the lorry so miserable was the rain that started that morning and then seemed to go on in an endless downpour from the skies. We had started off with a piece of plastic sheeting, but that was a disaster and we threw it away. So, having no cover, we were totally exposed and within minutes of a downpour we would be soaking wet.

UNITA had put grass in the bottom of the vehicle, and as the grass held the water it quickly became a soggy mess. As the rain continued, the back of the truck began to fill up with water. It was all sloshing around our feet, which were still septic, and our backsides. Only when the vehicle went uphill did it send a wave to the back, and some of the water would spill out. Otherwise it simply did not drain out fast enough.

After 37 or 38 hours of travelling in the truck, during which it was never dry, we must have had about 4 inches of water mixed with straw slushing around inside. And of course it wasn't only water and it wasn't only straw. Blokes would say: 'Stop, I have got to have a pee. I have got to have a pee.' But in the end it didn't matter any more, they just had to sit there and pee themselves. Some lads had diarrhoea, and they just could not get out. There are no two ways about it: we were a smelly mess even before we got into the vehicle but, once we were inside, the stench became worse and worse – almost unbearable. Travel sickness struck too. One young girl was vomiting. She tried to vomit over the side of the truck but caught some of us, so we had to put up with that as well.

The trouble was that we were so closely packed together

that we could not shift even when we had to pee or vomit or whatever. To start with we tried to arrange ourselves along the boxes of cargo that were piled down the centre of the vehicle and up both sides. When that did not work, we flattened the cargo out. One row of people would be sitting down one side of the vehicle with their backs to the headboard; then the next row would sit facing forwards with their legs open, and the next man would sit right tight into the preceding man's crutch. The next row would be facing the back with their legs open, pushed tight in. That was the way it was in theory; that was the way we would start off. But gradually UNITA, at the back, would keep packing us tighter, pushing us more and more to the front of the truck while some of them, the buggers, were lying out full-length – admittedly on top of one another, but taking up more space. And in any case whenever the vehicle hit a bump we would leave the floor of the vehicle and end up all skew-whiff and crushed in a heap.

It was hard-going, particularly with the UNITA women. There was one, aged about 20 or 22, sitting next to me, and she had monstrous breasts on her. It was John who was sitting pushed tight into her crutch and he had these monstrous breasts on either side of his head, like ear-muffs. She was complaining bitterly because she was so tightly packed in. Under normal circumstances, said John, it would have been quite pleasant. But she bitched and bitched all night, and there was nothing any of us could do to relieve her.

We still had septic feet, and all this vomit, straw and water with diarrhoea in it was sloshing around. Christ, we thought, what are our feet going to be like? For two days and nights they were never dry; and we had no idea of the state they might be in. To and fro it went, all sloshing about; it was really uncomfortable and unpleasant.

Four people rode in the vehicle cab: the driver, a spare driver (both maniacs – they never seemed to travel at less than 35-40 mph) and a UNITA captain and lieutenant. These were officers we had never seen before, and hardly knew, and by the fourth night we were getting a bit fed up with being treated like animals. We were becoming aggressive. The final straw was when they halted, that night, in a small base camp, and announced: 'You stay here for one hour only.'

I told all the Filipinos to get their blankets out and go to sleep; and then John, Paul, Al and myself had a bit of a confab. We agreed that we would hold out for better conditions. We had had enough. There was going to be a strike – a sort of mutiny.

About 3 a.m. the UNITA captain returned.

'Right,' he said, 'everybody back on the truck.'

'No,' we said. 'We are not getting on the truck. Either bring up another truck and divide the load or throw some of the people off.'

The UNITA captain was a bit nonplussed. He had breakfast served for us – tuna fish and rice, heated up, very pleasant – and then issued an ultimatum.

'Either you get into the truck,' he said, 'or I will order my men to force you.'

'You do what you like,' we said. 'But we are not getting into that truck.'

The Filipinos were getting a bit nervous at this confrontation.

'Lads,' I warned them, 'we all ought to stick together on this, else they will just hammer us into the ground. But you discuss it among yourselves first, and then give me your decision.'

So Roddy and Ephraim and a few of the other lads talked to everyone else. When they came back, the decision was that they agreed with us but that they did not want any trouble.

The UNITA captain, back again, tried his bullying tactics once more – and once more we turned him down. We simply went to sleep inside a large hut with a fire blazing. Outside it was absolutely teeming with rain.

At 6 a.m. UNITA trundled out the big brass – a lieutenant colonel we had never seen before and whom, we supposed, the junior officer had sent for so that he could sort us out.

'Now you will get back into this truck,' he ordered.

'No, we absolutely refuse,' we said. Roddy and myself were the spokesmen, and John and Paul both had a go at him. 'Not till we get more space,' we told him. 'You are treating us like animals.'

Up to this point the Captain had not said a word. But now he piped up: 'I think we should get in the vehicle and go.'

'No,' we replied. 'You can get in the vehicle and *you* can go if you like. But we are staying.'

He went out and consulted with the lieutenant colonel. We

couldn't hear what they were saying. A few minutes later the Captain came back into the hut again.

'UNITA have agreed that they will make some more space for us,' he announced.

We were absolutely stunned – shocked, you might say – because this was the first time the Captain had actually put himself out to assist us, his fellow hostages, in any way. What was more, he had succeeded in winning a concession. That concession led to others: first we insisted that all the cook women, about eight of them, be thrown off, together with their pots and pans. In return, as the officer said it was only about thirty hours' drive to Jamba, we agreed to eating only biscuits and water. Then the medic was to be removed; Roddy would look after us instead. Then, when we had won that point too, we insisted that three of the guards who had been particularly obnoxious and had slammed us around in the truck be taken off. The arguments raged backwards and forwards, but we were absolutely determined because the more we pushed, the more we seemed to be getting. Having won that point too, as it was still teeming with rain we demanded some tarpaulins.

'I think we are going too far,' said the Captain; and he went and sat in the truck by himself, getting soaking wet once again. But we refused – to give UNITA their due, they never tried to use force or violence, whatever their threats – and in the end, after more cafuffle, we had the pleasure of seeing tarpaulins brought out for us. So by standing on our rights as human beings we had won all the way down the line.

In the event, I have to admit that it turned out to be a bit of a Pyrrhic victory. Before, when the vehicle went round a corner, we had been packed in so tight that we could not move – as the truck leaned, we leaned. But now we had space between us and nothing to hang on to, particularly those of us who were sitting in the middle of the vehicle. So we were swaying this way and that, and falling over, and our backsides were really sore with the friction, particularly when the vehicle went over a bump. As it had two axles, one at the rear as well as one at the front, there would always be three separate jolts to jar us.

There was still vomit and diarrhoea swirling around under the tarpaulins but conditions were in general a slight improvement. I was standing up against the headboard – which was far more pleasant than sitting down. So I had a privileged position.

I spent something like eight hours on that stretch standing up and looking out over the cabin, occasionally turning round to shout out 'Watch your heads' when a branch came swishing by.

After eight hours we changed vehicles again, to an almost identical Russian-reconditioned vehicle that had been bringing ammunition boxes up from Jamba. It proved to have a far better engine – the previous one had been misfiring and banging – but it also had a new snag: the driver. We had thought the previous one was bad, but this one was a real maniac. Of course, the vehicle had more power. It could go faster, and he did go faster. He went like the clappers of hell.

The other snag was that because the sides of this new vehicle were higher – which was an improvement – the tarpaulin did not stretch right over the body, and a tug of war developed between the people in the centre, underneath, pushing it up to make a tent over them, and the people on the sides. The water was pouring off the tarpaulin straight on to them, or down their backs. Everybody was totally soaked, our blankets were soggy, and arguments were developing as the tarpaulin was hauled first one way and then the other.

'Sod it,' I said in the end, standing up and ripping this thing off. 'We do without. We can't get any wetter. Sod it.'

We stopped for a few minutes, changed drivers and then drove on right through the night, with the occasional pause to stretch our legs. The rain had ceased, and the UNITA officers escorting us were showing a bit more consideration. We were starting to dry out, though the wind was cold.

At about two in the morning, passing through very dense bush, Al stood up.

'I want to go to the toilet,' he said, 'and I am not going to sit in this goddam truck doing it in my breeches.'

So he and I started banging on the cabin roof, and, as the vehicle stopped, Al was over the side. He rushed into the long grass, dropped his trousers and got on with it.

The UNITA captain emerged sleepily from the truck cab. 'What's the problem?' he asked.

'It is just Al,' we said. 'He has diarrhoea.'

'Where is he?'

'Out there in the grass.'

'But there are lions out there! We are in lion country.'

For a moment we were stunned. Then we yelled, 'Al, come back! It's lion country!'

And back came Al roaring out of the bush with his trousers dangling down around his ankles.

Shortly afterwards, without further misadventure, we reached a camp. At this stage we were so exhausted that we simply slept for an hour or two on the ground.

They woke us long before dawn; we drove on till past dawn, when we pulled into a small village. We were herded into a hut with – thankfully – a fire in it, and there we dozed off again. The ordeal in the back of the truck, the lack of sleep and the lack of food since the last rest-day had worn us down physically and mentally; tempers were now very short. But, as always seemed to happen when we were at our lowest ebb, UNITA pulled something out of the hat. This time it was a Land Rover that careered up at about 6 a.m. An interesting-looking box was unloaded from the back.

'Look at that,' somebody exclaimed. 'That is bloody bread!'

It was. There were two slices of bread for everybody in that treasure-chest of a box, rough white bread, and a slice of cheese, and coffee again, mugs of hot milky coffee. It was the first cheese and the first bread we had seen, and it was absolutely fantastic: UNITA had sent this Land Rover up from Jamba specially with our breakfast. We sat around the fire nursing our mugs of coffee and our cheese sandwiches, absolutely chuffed. About fifteen minutes went by and we were snuggling down ready to have another sleep when they called us out again. This time they gave each of us a whole pear and a whole peach plus juice in the mugs in which we had had coffee – tinned pears and peaches they were, delicious. Morale shot up something fantastic. It shot up even more when they told us we were only five hours' drive from Jamba. This time, as breakfast had been sent out from there, what could we do but believe them?

As we piled back into the truck, we found a Portuguese sitting in one of the corners whom we had never seen before. He was well-dressed; he had a good jacket on, trousers, shoes, and he was carrying a type of sailor's kit-bag full of mail.

'Where have you come from?' we asked.

'I have been a prisoner since November,' he said. 'I was captured in Lucapa.'

It turned out that he had been captured by UNITA as he

was travelling from Dundo to Lucapa. He was a Diamang employee and he had been carrying all the company's mail – which UNITA had allowed him to keep all this time and which John eventually delivered to the offices in Johannesburg. He had been shot through the back of the leg and the tendons to his foot had been cut, so his foot just flopped about on the end of his leg. Apart from that, he looked quite fit; indeed, he was a lot fitter than the rest of us because he had been carried almost all the way. He was delighted to see us – we were the first whites he had seen since his capture four months earlier – and the other four Portuguese, Bushbunny included, were all blathering away within moments: who are you, where have you been, this that and the other. I was a bit less welcoming, I'm afraid, because he was sitting in my corner place.

'Move your arse out of there,' I said.

He moved his arse; and off we went. Soon it was teeming with rain again. 'Sod it,' we thought, 'we can stand this, we've only got four or five hours more now.' But fate, and UNITA's driving, had it in for us once again. After five hours – during which we passed very close by a group of nine ostriches – we stopped for lunch and were told we had only five more hours to go – '*a typical example of UNITA estimation and logical thinking*,' Paul wrote indignantly in the diary. Going on again after lunch, still in the rain, we came to a fork in the track, and there was a signpost. It was the first signpost we had seen on the whole journey; and one of the directions indicated was Jamba. The driver, however, took the wrong fork. He realized his mistake, swung the wheel round and set off across country to rejoin the right track – and became bogged down with both axles in a mire of running sand.

I won't describe all the efforts that were made to get the vehicle out of that sand. At first we just enjoyed standing there, in little streams of water, with the rain washing the muck off us. Then, as UNITA were only succeeding in getting the truck stuck deeper and deeper, we took a hand, using a fallen tree as a lever.

This UNITA officer came over to me.

'Look, you are too old,' he told me. 'You are an old man. You go and stand away from it.'

My beard by this time was about three inches long and silvery grey. I suppose that made me look older. But I felt quite insulted.

'You cheeky young sod,' I said. 'Get out of the way.'

But all the UNITA lads came crowding around, quite concerned.

'No, you go away,' they said. 'Maybe you damage yourself.' And they went on and on.

'Oh well, sod it,' I thought. I hauled a tarpaulin over a bush to make a tent, cut some branches with a machete, took some diesel from the fuel tank and managed to get a fire going. So I sulked with the Captain and the older men, like Achilles in his tent, while one hour went by, two hours went by, three hours went by – and the mistake they were making was to jack up one axle and pack stuff under it while the other two axles just went deeper and deeper kicking out all the stuff from under them.

In the end I could stand it no longer. I went across and told them to sod off. Then I got all the young Filipinos together.

'Look, lads,' I said, 'do it this way. Go round all the axles, pack all the axles, then cut branches and make a mattress 20-30 feet long, so when the vehicle does come out it won't sink back into the sand again.'

I had given my advice: it was up to them to take it or leave it. I went back to the fire, to try and dry myself out again, one side at a time. When I had my back to the vehicle I suddenly heard this tremendous cheer. Out it had lurched and now it was standing on firm ground again. Everyone was dancing up and down in joy because we had almost given up hope of getting to Jamba that day. Jamba was becoming a mirage, always just within reach, so to speak, but always disappearing out of reach again the closer we seemed to get to it.

We piled back into the truck. It rained for the next hour, then it eased off at about tea-time – not that we had any tea – then it started teeming down again as dusk approached. Soon we were driving through floods, with the water over the top of the vehicle's wheels and the exhaust pipe making glub-glub-glub sounds under water. The headlights reflected nothing but water and how the driver knew where the hell he was going we could not imagine, because it was just like a lake. He was in first gear, using all the 6-wheel drive, and it took him about two hours in the darkness to get through these floods.

It was cold, bitterly cold, by the time we emerged on to the track again. We were soaking wet, it was raining, Jamba did not seem to be coming any nearer, there were unexplained stops and starts, and we were becoming really dejected.

Crossing another flooded area, the vehicle stalled. 'Oh Jesus, no,' we thought. But the driver shifted quickly into reverse and we pulled out safely. Further on swamps encompassed us; we were really surprised at the amount of traction that vehicle had, and how it got us through the swamps.

All of a sudden we were driving through dense bush again. Then we came out into clearer country, where all the ground was sand, pure sand, with chunks of grass and trees in it. An archway loomed up in our headlights. Beside it a man was standing with a check-board. He checked us off. After five minutes we moved off. A little further on we pulled up by a big hut. The UNITA captain got out and came round.

'Right, lads,' he said, 'this is Jamba.'

Bleeding hell, we thought, where is the town? Where is the capital? Where is our brick-built house? Where the hell *is* Jamba?

Chapter VIII

Jamba

'Where the hell is Jamba?' we repeated out loud to the major who welcomed us.

'This is Jamba,' he said, spreading his hands.

'We were given the impression it was a big town.'

'It *is* a big town.'

We were baffled as well as disappointed. We were separated into four groups: British, Americans, Filipinos and Portuguese; and each group was led off in a different direction. John, Paul and I were escorted in a northerly direction, to a grass hut with electric light and beds – steel-framed army beds with thick mattresses.

'How long do we stay here?' we asked the major.

'You stay here,' he said – he spoke excellent English, which was just as well as there was no Francis with us now to interpret Portuguese for us – 'You stay here till you are released by UNITA.'

'How long will that be?'

'I don't know, but this will be your home.'

We were standing in puddles of water, wrapped in wet blankets and soaked through. It was well after midnight.

'Take off all your clothes,' said the major.

We obeyed. We stripped off and were left standing there in the nudy, each feeling a bit of a fool. There were two stooges standing by the beds, dressed in military denims. We were told that they would be our stewards. They brought us a pair of slacks each, and a shirt, Bermuda-type underpants, a pair of socks, some plimsolls and a towel.

'Dry off and get into bed,' said the Major.

We dried off, and we got into bed. The two stewards brought us big thermoses of coffee, tins of condensed milk and a big bowl of sugar, with a spoon each and a plastic cup, then an aluminium bowl of fried potatoes and corned beef. We dived into that, barely listening to the major as he wished us 'Happy dreams'. Then I tripped the light out and went out like a light myself. So did John and Paul. We were absolutely dead to the world.

Our encampment was in effect a small village. We were confined to this area for about three weeks and during that time we had no idea what was around us. It was a queer situation, being separated nationality-wise. The Portuguese were in the west, the Americans were in the east, we were in the north, and the Filipinos had two grass-built huts in the south. In the centre of the camp complex was a hut for four UNITA officers – one for each nationality, the major being in charge of us, the British.

For the first couple of days all we were interested in was relaxing. Then I wanted to see what the Filipinos' quarters were like and how they were faring.

'No,' said the major, 'you are not allowed in that part of the camp.'

They did not like us to communicate with one another. They did not want us mixing.

'Why?' I would ask.

'Because your treatment is different from the Filipinos'.'

'O.k., I want to see in what way.'

'Your treatment is better.'

'They are my Filipinos,' I would retort. 'I want to see them.' And so the argument would go on, inconclusively.

The result was that I would sneak through the bush and pay the Filipinos a visit at night. There were no armed guards or anything like that; indeed even the UNITA officers never carried weapons, except perhaps when visitors like lieutenant colonels or brigadiers came; and then the major would buckle on his pistol. So there was no real constraint. But the encampment was very scattered; the Filipinos' huts were a good fifteen minutes' walk away.

In fact the difference in our treatment consisted mainly in food, which went down through the ranks nationality-wise. The British and the Americans were absolutely force-fed. Breakfast was at about 7 a.m., lunch at 12 noon and the evening meal about 6 p.m. We could ask for anything we wanted; and if UNITA had it, they would give it to us. So some mornings we would have freshly-made doughnuts with big 2-lb tins of jam – the only snag being that all the labels were off the tins, so we might have to open up three, perhaps, before finding marmalade.

'Why do these tins come with no labels on?' we asked.

'We buy them cheaper that way,' was the answer.

But it was not the real reason. The real reason we found on the toilet rolls: stamped on the end of them was 'S.A.', and in fact unmarked helicopters were flying in supplies from South Africa at least once a week. One or two would land at about 10 p.m. in the dark and would leave again, also in utter darkness, at about 4 a.m. They would land about a mile or so away from us on a football pitch, and their take-off would wake us up. This made us suspect that they were hedge-hopping in from Namibia and getting back again before daylight. The next morning we would have entirely fresh food: meat, doughnuts, fish and so on; then the quality of the food would gradually tail off until the next helicopter landing.

We had milk and rice boiled, or condensed milk and rice boiled, we would have chips (we showed the cook how to do chips), meat not that often, butter, biscuits, the occasional bottle of wine, the occasional can of beer; and when we arrived the major presented the three of us with a bottle of whisky. We were on a fattening programme; they wanted to fatten us up.

Myself, I always like to carry extra weight in Africa, because if you get a bad dose of, for instance, malaria you can easily lose half a stone. When I was in Ethiopia and had typhus, I lost about seven stone; if I had not been overweight I might easily have died, the medic there informed me. I had weighed 17 stone and I ended up at 9 stone 1 lb; and all that within four weeks. It had taken me two weeks to get to a hospital because I was right in the middle of the Danakil desert when I caught typhus. So I was overweight when I was captured by UNITA, which was just as well seeing that, although it was no typhus scare, I lost easily two stone on the march.

But in Jamba I think we probably put back on a stone each. To begin with, we had boiled rice and pilchards most days till we absolutely refused to eat any more. A senior officer was summoned, a lieutenant colonel.

'What is the problem?' he said. 'Why will you not eat the food?'

'We are fed up with the bloody stuff,' we replied. 'We want something else, some variety.'

'O.k. What do you want?'

'We want chips, we want eggs, we want steak, we want . . .' and on it went.

In a way we were just bitching because we were bored. I think we caused more problems for UNITA in Jamba than at any other time during our journey down (except for the occasion of our 'mutiny' on – or, rather, off – the lorry).

But when we got, for instance, fried potatoes and tuna fish, the Portuguese would only get macaroni, or perhaps sardines. We would have coffee and tea; they did not. We had perhaps two packets of cigarettes a day between the three of us, and they would have one pack a day between the five of them.

Bushbunny, though, was in heaven – perhaps because it was years since he had had good food and regular meals at all. It was certainly the first time he had ever slept on a real steel bed. The other Portuguese used to come down to our hut and tell us the sort of things he did. Whenever they had mashed potatoes and minced meat – their regular diet – he would gorge himself, so much that he would vomit it all up, only to start again because he did not want under any circumstances to miss his fill. Quite often, as a result, he would be rolling around in pain from over-eating. But after two or three weeks his stomach grew so distended that he could have swallowed a horse. I would say that, when captured, he probably weighed somewhere around 8½ stone, 9 stone maximum; but after a few weeks in Jamba he must have been somewhere around 11 stone, with a big belly, two chins, the lot.

As conditions relaxed, Al used to come over to our hut frequently. He used to come in the morning for a coffee. He was a comedian, he really was. He would come walking up, and from the position I lay in on my bed I could see directly out of the door to the pathway he would approach by. As soon as I clapped eyes on him, I'd say: 'Top of the morning. Here's that goddam Yank again.'

'Hi, you Brits,' he'd shout. 'How ya doing?'

That was his greeting every morning. We used to sit and talk and he would ramble on, and we would have some good laughs. He also came up every afternoon – mainly to have a break from the Captain.

One evening we had told the cook boy: 'Tomorrow for breakfast we want bread, cheese and butter.' Off the lad went and, blow me, next morning we got Red Leicestershire Cheese, which I love, a big block of it, with bread and butter. A bit later Al came up.

'Hi, you guys, how ya doing?' he said. 'Whadya have for breakfast?'

'Bread, butter and cheese,' we told him.

'Cheese? There ain't no cheese.'

'We had cheese.' we repeated.

He went back and told the Captain. The Captain stalked over to the cookhouse, and there was a rumpus, a flaming row.

'But,' said the cook to the Captain, 'you never said you wanted cheese!'

After this, every time Al came over and asked us 'Whadya have for dinner?' we would reply 'roast chicken' or 'steak' or something like that for him to report back to the Captain.

In the end the cook got fed up with this and came across to us.

'For Christ's sake,' he said, 'don't make any more trouble for me, because I have that Captain on my back all the time saying I don't give him this and I do give you that, and so on.'

So we had to pack it in. The Captain had no sense of humour at all. As for Al, he was totally submissive; anything the Captain said he should do, he did. The Captain liked to go to bed at 8 o'clock in the evening; so at 8 o'clock in the evening Al would go to bed. He did not like Al to smoke inside their grass hut, so Al would have to go outside to smoke. They had a radio between them; Al can't stand opera but the Captain always wanted opera, so opera it was. He was as soft as muck, was Al. We all used to say to him: 'Al, you are an idiot. Just get your bed and move it up into our house.' But he would not do it. I think he thought the Captain could do him a lot of damage as regards his flying career.

Our own relations with the Captain over this period in Jamba went from bad to worse. Take, for example, the bottle of whisky the major had given us on arrival, to be shared between us three British and the two Americans.

'Let's keep the whisky till we have something to celebrate,' we suggested. 'No point in just throwing it down our throats.'

'I don't agree with that because I don't drink,' said the Captain.

'I don't drink either,' I said, 'so I've got no designs on the whisky myself. But I think it is better to keep it for an occasion.'

'Well, now is an occasion,' he said. 'Let's have a tot in our coffee.'

'O.k.,' John and Paul agreed. 'A good idea.'

As I had said I didn't drink, I took normal coffee myself, without whisky. But the Captain poured out about half an inch of coffee in the bottom of his tin mug and filled the rest of it up with whisky, despite having claimed that he did not drink. That was the sort of hypocritical behaviour he indulged in. Everyone just watched him amazed. 'Cretin!' they exclaimed. It made no difference to him.

Then there were the cigarettes. When we got to Jamba he told the UNITA lads: 'I don't smoke, I don't need cigarettes.'

This meant that we lost some cigarettes as a group, and that really irritated us.

'Dirty habit!' he would say whenever he saw one of us smoking.

'It is just the same for you, with your pills,' we would answer.

We tried to be pleasant with him but he was too difficult a character to get on with. He never put himself out to visit us and we didn't put ourselves out to visit him; but sometimes we would go down and see Al, and so we would see him as well. We would have a crack but if he was obnoxious we would let rip. In the end we just did not bother about him at all because to talk to him was exactly like talking to a brick wall – predictable.

So life was very difficult for Al. But the three of us in our hut got on exceptionally well, fortunately. I was more the odd one out because I was a lot older. So I was probably the most stable one among the three of us and, having been in the army, where you are messed about from pillar to post and spend 90 per cent of your time just hanging about, I can pass my time quite peacefully just by myself. Paul was the chatterbox; he needed company and he needed to chatter. But he was short of subjects. He could talk a bit about Ethiopia and bits of work he had done in the UK and school life; and that was about it. But he had no hobbies, so he was soon stumped. He strangled every bit of information just for something to talk about; and if there was a laugh that could be screwed out of any subject, then he would do it.

John was a very quiet lad, and he had no – or very little – sense of humour. Never did he tell a joke in all the time we were together. But Paul and John, as their ages were closer, had a lot more to talk about in the way of films and pop stars. In particular they would discuss films that they had both seen, and they would go on with these conversations for hours on end. As I had been in Africa for fourteen years, I had not had much chance to see films; and in any case I am not a film-goer; so I would say nothing. 'Let's talk about Tony Hancock,' Paul would crack, looking at my glum face and knowing that I liked Tony Hancock. But there was no bad feeling.

Even those two would talk themselves into a stupor eventually and there would be long pauses, of about two or three hours, in which we didn't say anything because there was nothing to say. At other times, though, we would talk about star signs, religion and politics, and history, too – modern history is one of my interests; and we would argue with John about South Africa's politics. When I first met him I had not been able to figure out John's nationality; I would never have taken him for an Irish South African. But at Jamba his Irish brogue came out when he talked about Ireland, and we learnt a lot from him about Ulster and the IRA. John is no fool; he is very intelligent. We used to bait him and say, 'That is Paddy-land over there'; but he never took offence. In those six weeks in Jamba, between the three of us, we must have exhausted every possible topic of conversation.

The sheer boredom of that period was unreal. After the first two weeks Paul had a tantrum.

'I'm fed up and I want to go home,' he cried.

'You can't just go into the bush,' we reasoned with him. 'You are stuck, and you have to put up with it.'

'I can't put up with it any more,' he shouted. 'I'm going round the bend. I'm going daft.' He ranted on for about two hours, throwing things around and being generally obnoxious.

'O.k.,' we said, 'what do you want to do?'

'I am going to walk out of this place!'

'Where are you going to walk to? There *is* nowhere to walk to!'

It took a lot to settle him down.

Even John, though he was such a quiet lad, came near to breaking-point on one occasion. Our two stewards had little huts behind ours, about 30 yards away, and one of their jobs was to keep an eye on us and make sure that we did not stray. Just for a joke we decided to have them on. We said to the stewards: 'After lunch we are going for a walk. We are going to look for women.'

After lunch the steward on duty was sitting at the door of his hut, watching us. I came out of the back door and started heading east. Then he saw Paul and John coming out of the front door, John heading north and Paul heading south. As agreed, we were all making off in different directions.

This steward got in a right tizzwazz. In the end he was just running round in circles screaming, 'Major! Major!' Ten minutes later John and I met up at the Portuguese hut, and the major and some of his men came storming in to hustle us back.

That was it. John really let fly at him. 'You black bastard,' he said, and he effed and he blinded. He was very upset – near to tears. I was trying to calm him down, but this slanging match went on for about five minutes with the major not saying very much at all. In the end we all drifted back to our hut. So what had started off as a joke ended in disaster. The major, who had been good to us, now had the hump. It took a few days for us to get back on pally terms with him, and John had to apologize for swearing at him and insulting him. It had been a dodgy moment.

But in general we struck up some good relationships with UNITA. Our other steward had been shot in a battle with SWAPO*, and as the muscles underneath his jaw were gone and he was incapable of carrying anything on his head, he had been invalided out of active service. He was quite an intelligent guy, and a comic. We would try to take the mickey out of him.

'The food is no good, the house is no good, the electric light is no good,' we would say. 'There are no women, no booze, no music – and this is Jamba, the capital of UNITA! What a bunch of wallies you lot are.'

'All you do,' he would retort, 'is live in a concrete jungle. You didn't know what a bloody tree was before you came to Angola and I think you had never seen a cow before in your lives.'

So we had some good laughs with him. UNITA never tried to humiliate us in any way – unlike some of the Nigerians I have worked with, who are really aggressive, racist types, and who would have loved to have had us in that situation.

In the whole time we were at Jamba it only rained twice; and, though it was often overcast, the highlight of our day was sunbathing. Jamba was teeming with beautiful tropical birds and once, as I was lying sunbathing, a bird looking a bit like a robin but with a longer beak and tail came out of a little thicket

*The South West Africa People's Organization – the guerrillas fighting the South African army in Namibia. They were based in Angola and were supported by the Marxist government, so they also fought against UNITA.

and hopped around in the sand beside me picking up ants. It hopped up on to my chest and balanced there; I lay very still, not moving an eyeball, till it moved across and disappeared back into the thicket again.

We would sunbathe in the nudy, and we got so used to it that we just didn't give a damn. The worst that happened was that sometimes these UNITA lads might point to our family jewels and say: '*Pequeno* – very small!'

'Yes,' we'd say. 'Black man, all his brains are down there, that is why he is so big,' making a joke of it. So it was no real hassle.

A lieutenant colonel came round to inspect us; and we complained bitterly about the boredom.

'O.k.,' he said. 'I'll try and organize something. What would you like?'

'Books, newspapers . . . anything.'

They brought us some books; and we read them from cover to cover. They were probably from Savimbi's own library. There were some books that were really hard-going, physics and stuff like that, which we could not get into. There was volume II of *The History of the English-speaking Peoples* by Winston Churchill and *Memorandum on the Second World War*, also by Churchill. There was *My Wicked, Wicked Ways* by Errol Flynn; and one Wilbur Smith book entitled, suitably enough, *Gold Mine*. The trouble was that I'd read it before, and it wasn't one of his best books either; but I read it again twice. My problem is that I am long-sighted; and as UNITA had stamped on my glasses at capture, I could read in the daytime with the book near my feet but I could not read at night by the light of the 60-watt bulb in the roof.

As regards newspapers, we were given from time to time outdated copies of *Time* magazine, about 3-4 months old, and the impression we got was that *Time* covered UNITA better than any other paper. From newspaper comments, and from the way the British Ambassador in Angola, in Luanda, spoke about him, we received the impression that Jonas Savimbi, UNITA's president, was a gentleman. The ambassador never slagged Savimbi off, though he was accredited to his enemies. So, by adding all these things up together, we gathered that Savimbi was quite a civilized, intelligent, human guy; and certainly we had no fear of being exterminated. Whereas if we had fallen into the hands of any other guerrilla group – no way!

We were given badminton bats and balls, too, but we did not play because it was hard-going in the sand and we were not really interested in physical exercise. The Filipinos played badminton though, and also chess. Indeed they organized a champion chess tournament that took eight days to run. Then we had the board between us; but I don't play chess and John, who is a good chess-player, beat Paul every time they played. So that soon palled.

The highlight of the day came to be the fly-kill. 'Right, lads, exercise time,' I would say; and all three of us would dive off our beds and kill flies for an hour. We would probably get the whole room down to two surviving flies, which was all to the good, as during the day we were plagued with flies.

There were plenty of bark spiders in our hut to give us a hand with this job. They were about as thick as a penny, and they were called bark spiders because they would penetrate under the bark of trees to winkle the insects out. Unfortunately Paul had a phobia about spiders. Every time a spider came down from our grass roof on to the floor he would go rigid, then dive out of bed and kill it.

One nice warm morning – overcast but warm – we were lying on our beds and Paul was chattering away. All of a sudden he went quiet. I spoke and he just grunted.

'What's the matter with you, you pillock?' I asked.

'Aaah,' he said.

'All right, don't bloody talk then,' I said, disgruntled.

I turned over to face him. His finger came up in a jerky motion just a few inches above his rigid body. Two or three feet above him was a snake dangling down from the bamboo walls. She had her head and about ten inches of her body out: beautiful colours. Her tongue was flicking but I could see that she was harmless as she had a very slim head.

'It's all right, Paul,' I said. 'It's not poisonous.'

He was up and off his bed in a flash. We tried to catch the snake but it retreated behind the plastic that lined our roof; and there it spent the night hunting the rats and the mice who lived in the roof and who would start moving about as soon as we switched the electric light off. Occasionally we whacked at them with our badminton bats, just for a bit of peace; and occasionally they would come down on the floor and pick up crumbs as we lay there and watched them.

So there was rustling up above all that night, and Paul could not sleep for fear that the snake might come down from the roof again – whereas I slept well because in general snakes don't bother me. In Nigeria I once caught a young rock python, down in a quarry. He was only 3 foot 6 inches long, and I thought he would make a decent pet if I took him home. He did, and we kept him around the house for three months. The only trouble was that we kept losing him; we would have to have an all-out hunt and would find him behind the bookcase or wrapped around a Coca-Cola bottle. He had a knack of slipping under the lounge door, even though he was 3 inches in diameter and there was only a 1-inch gap. Pythons are only dangerous when they are big; and he was much less dangerous than a rhesus monkey we also had as a pet. He was called Toby, and was about two feet tall. Monkeys can be very destructive. One weekend Toby wrecked the canteen, then she went into the workshop and ripped all the insides out of a Mercedes car, a Toyota jeep and a Mercedes grease truck. I had had enough, so I destroyed her.

Even big pythons are only dangerous when they are hungry; but as they eat only once every three or four months that isn't often. Once in Nigeria, at night, driving along, I came across an enormous python blocking the road. I stopped the jeep and got out to shift him, but I could not even get my hands around his body. He must have been 7 or 8 inches across.

The only snakes I do not trust are spitting cobras and black mambas. The puff adder is a dangerous one, too, but 90 per cent of snakes will turn and make off when they see you, and leave you alone. I came across all sorts of snakes in Nigeria, including these three species; but the most extraordinary sight I ever saw there was at Kaduna, where we were asphalting the main runway of the international airport. We would lay asphalt about 4 inches thick, having cleared the topsoil away for half a mile on either side. Work would finish at 8 p.m. each night, and as the job continued into the rainy season, the nights turned cold. Many a time I would get into my jeep at night and drive alongside the hot asphalt that had been laid earlier that day; and there on it were snakes all over the place, come to keep themselves warm; and I am talking about hundreds of pythons, puff adders, adders, any species you care to think of. God knows where they came from. It was a most weird, impressive sight.

We had been three weeks or so at Jamba, the rainy season had come to an end and it was warm, so we slept with only a sheet to cover us. It was about 2 or 3 a.m., and I was lying fast asleep with my arm hanging out of the bed probably 2 or 3 inches off the floor. Suddenly something wet came and touched my arm just above the wrist. Automatically I jerked my arm up – and hit whatever it was, the muzzle of which had touched me in the chest, between the front legs. It toppled over on its back, scrambled up, roared across the room, tried to go out of the front door, hit the net curtain, tangled itself up, catapulted back into the room, and finally escaped.

'What was that?' said Paul, waking up.

'I think it was a fox.'

'They don't have foxes in Africa,' said Paul, scornfully.

At that very moment a second fox shot out from under my bed, and did the same thing with the door and the curtain; as we switched on the electric light, we caught a glimpse of it. It was a small animal with a bushy tail, so it was certainly either a fox or a blackbat jackal.

But it was not the most sinister of our visitors. Two or three nights later I was lying on my bed – it was about 9 p.m. – and an awful stench came up right next to me. The walls of the hut were bamboo, so the breeze used to blow straight through.

John's bed was next to mine.

'What the hell is that?' he said.

'It stinks like hyena to me,' I said.

Hyenas will roll in rotting carcasses; and it was that sort of smell. Then it must have walked towards Paul because he smelt it.

Every two or three days a gang of lads would come around at dawn, all singing and whistling and shouting, making a dreadful din, and sweep the area around our hut. We used to insult them rotten for waking us up. So next morning I went out, saw these footprints, and did quite a bit of mileage around the house, following the tracks.

'A hyena has been sniffing around here, definitely,' I said.

'No,' said the major, who had – inevitably – come up. 'A dog.'

'A funny-looking dog that is,' I retorted, 'with small feet at the back.

A hyena always walks a little bit at an angle, and the pads are bigger at the front than they are at the back. Their tracks were familiar to me because of my experiences with them in Ethiopia; and afterwards, for a few nights, on my advice, no one would go out of our hut for a jimmy riddle in the dark.

Though a single hyena is not dangerous, they are very peculiar, unpredictable animals. One long-ago night in Ethiopia, in the Danakil desert, we saw a trail of blood and bits of flesh leading off the road towards the ditch. I am always inquisitive, so Wolde pulled up the jeep. A camel that looked as if a truck had hit it was lying in the ditch, with its back leg ripped off and shattered in the road. A pack of hyenas was trying to tear its stomach out, and the camel was still moaning and grunting as it lay there.

I knew it was nature's way, but all the same it disgusted me. So, as I had always heard that hyenas were cowardly beasts, I started throwing stones at them and, sure enough, they backed off about 5 or 6 feet away. 'We'll put this poor bugger out of his misery,' I said to Wolde.

So I unholstered my Beretta .22, went up to the camel's head, and shot it. But the bullet hit a boney knob and ricocheted off. So the next time I shot it through the eye, straight up into the brain, and killed it. I wasn't watching the hyenas, because I had always had the impression that they were very timid animals. But when I turned round, it was to find the whole pack of them advancing on me.

'Bugger this,' I thought, panicking. I picked up a stone, threw it and hit one. But the brute did not back off. I scrambled hurriedly up the bank. The hyenas didn't stop at the dead camel. They clambered over it and came on up after me. I was between the headlights and they still didn't stop. They swarmed right up around the jeep, though fortunately by this time I was safely inside, mopping my brow. I later heard of an American Peace Corps lad who had been in the Ogaden, sleeping, when a hyena took the whole of the side of his face off. So personally I would always be wary of hyenas, particularly in packs. I consider them very dangerous animals.

Not far from our big hut was a small, round hut, with a hole in the ground and a grass roof over it, that served as a loo; one morning Paul came running from it with his trousers around his ankles, having seen yet another snake – a grass snake this time. Quite tame it was; it just looked at us and sauntered off (very different from the black mamba that once nearly caught me in the same position behind some rocks in northern Nigeria and had me running for my life, as I pointed out to the lad).

For washing we had a big tin bath outside, full of water which we would chuck over ourselves. That was quite serviceable, but it did not cover all our personal hygiene requirements.

'Can we have a toothbrush?' we asked.

'No, there are no toothbrushes,' we were told.

'Well, can we shave? Can you get us a razor?'

'No, we can't do that,' came the discouraging reply.

Fortunately, close to the Americans' hut stood another in which some Portuguese and Italian priests who had also been taken hostage were living. Al got friendly with them and they had one razor, an old Gillette with a screw-on handle. The priests lent Al this razor. He shaved his beard off, Paul shaved his off except for a moustache, and I was the third – and last – to use it, as John did not want to shave at all. By this time the blade was pretty blunt and, having no mirror, I shaved with the sugar bowl, which was chrome. I almost ripped my face off; but two inches of grey beard came with it; and once this had gone I really felt great. But still not being able to clean one's teeth, after over two months, was really irritating.

It was in the first days of March, about four weeks after our arrival at Jamba, that the major rolled up, about midday.

'Get ready, get dressed,' he said. 'You are going on a trip.'

'When?' we asked.

'In one hour's time.'

By this time we had been on a tour or two outside our encampment, and had a general idea of what Jamba was like. It was totally spread out and largely underground, so it presented no proper target to FAPLA bombers or any other attacking force. The hospital, for instance, was spread over half a square mile, with no two buildings connected; and the operating theatre was an underground bunker. When we were first shown round it, we were taken into the maternity ward there; our guide swung the curtains back and there was a woman on stirrups with her baby's head just appearing between her legs. 'I want to be off,' I said. It was impressive but not my scene. I felt really queasy.

On another occasion they had taken us on a VIP-style guided tour of the armoury. If we had not been taken we would never have known the armoury was there, as it was very well camouflaged and half underground. Sixty-five to 70 per cent of the equipment, including a lot of anti-aircraft guns, was Russian or Czech and had been captured from FAPLA or SWAPO. UNITA also had tanks and armoured cars, all captured, and antiquated Russian 6-wheel trucks, hundreds of them. There seemed to be no shortage of fuel at all, no economy measures – a thing that puzzled us greatly – and it was all diesel. They even washed the trucks down in diesel.

The main problem with Jamba was that it was built on very fine white sand, which meant that the vehicles all had to use 4-wheel drive. The main roads were covered with branches, especially laid down for the purpose. There was street lighting, but it only functioned in the central area, where the open-air theatre was and where there were 20 or 30 buildings grouped together – a possible target; the street lighting was only switched on when VIPs, in particular the foreign press, paid a visit. It had all been looted and brought down from Cafunfo and other places in the north.

The main UNITA forces were living about a mile away from us, in grass huts all spread out under the trees. We were told that they received no salary but were issued with clothes and food for themselves and their families. Anything else they might want, like a radio, was issued on a merit system; and most of the goodies of life had to be acquired when they went out on raids.

We had already been taken to the central area to be shown an hour-long video film of UNITA tactics, with their lads fighting and capturing Cubans and Czechs, so we imagined this visit would be just another of those shows – or possibly a propaganda rally – and we were not overly excited. So we dressed, and were collected by lorry, and were then driven to the central area, to a big, open hut with seats all the way round and room for about 60 or 70 people.

What gave us an inkling that this might be something different was when first one, then another, then a third Land Rover drew up and disgorged not the usual hooligans but guards, smartly dressed, with creases in their trousers, armed with brand-new AK 47s and high-powered hunting rifles. They deployed themselves all round the hut and into the bush.

Then a new 4-wheel-drive Mercedes pulled up, and out of it stepped Jonas Savimbi.

All the way down, throughout the long march, we had been

given soft soap by UNITA: 'The reason you must walk fast,' they were always saying, 'is that our leader is waiting for you. He is standing there waiting for you in Jamba.' So when we arrived we had been keyed up at first, expecting to meet him. Then the initial two or three days went by, and we thought, 'He is just letting us rest.' But as the days merged into weeks we put it down, if we thought about it at all, to just another UNITA ploy. So when Jonas Savimbi finally appeared, it came as a total surprise.

In the flesh he was stocky, bearded, and he had a definite air of authority about him. He was wearing a beret and military uniform. His shoes were highly polished, and there wasn't a speck on them – or him. All his lieutenant colonels, his council, were there with him – and to our surprise they all spoke good English.

He led the way into the big hut, and we were then invited to go in one by one, first the Americans, then the British, then the Portuguese, then the Filipinos. He shook hands with all of us; we sat down round him, in a circle, with his council on one side.

President Savimbi spoke very good English himself, though with a German accent because all his education had been in Switzerland.

'First of all,' he said, 'I am going to try and answer the question that is uppermost in your minds: release. You will be released as soon as the Red Cross can organize it. When that will be I don't know. It could be next week, it could be the week after. All depends on the Red Cross.'

We discovered, later, that this was not strictly true. It was the Red Cross who were waiting for UNITA to give them the go-ahead, and they were not informed that they could come in until four days before we were actually released. The President was in fact deliberately holding us back for a big publicity stunt, to tie in with the nineteenth anniversary of the foundation of UNITA, due to be celebrated a couple of weeks later.

Then he launched into his tale of woe: 'You people have caused me a lot of problems,' he said. 'Great,' I thought; 'What have you caused us?' 'You were not supposed to be in Cafunfo at all. But once we had captured you, we could not release you for fear that FAPLA might kill you and blame it on us. So we had to transport you all the way down to Jamba. We had to send special troops to act as your escort, and we had to get special food in because you don't like the local food. All you people have cost me a fortune.'

He went on to tell us, deadpan, exactly how the operation had first gone wrong.

'My lieutenant colonel came up on the radio on 27 December,' he said. 'He told me he had reconnoitred Cafunfo and that there were no expatriates at all living there. "O.k.," I told him, "make a dawn attack on the 28th." In fact he delayed the attack till Saturday; and on Saturday morning, the 29th, at 9 a.m., he came up on the radio again. "Boss," he said, "there are a few problems." "Well," I said, "what are they?" "I have just captured two Britons." "I thought you said there were no expatriates in Cafunfo." "We thought there weren't but we made a mistake and there were." "Take them out about 10 kilometres into the bush, keep them there, and I will contact you." "Boss," he said, "there is another small problem. We have captured 17 Filipinos as well, and three Portuguese." "O.k., get them into the bush, get them out of Cafunfo." Later on, about 2 or 3 p.m., that lieutenant colonel called me up again. "I have another problem," he began. "I have made a bit of a mistake." "You can't make any more mistakes," I said, disbelievingly. "It's been a disaster already. What have you done now?" "I have shot an American aeroplane down." "You've what?" "I have shot an American aeroplane down," he repeated. "You can't have shot an American aeroplane down," I said. "There are no American aeroplanes there. Only – " (I paused) "Trans-American." "Yes," he said, "that is the one we shot down." "Are there any survivors?" "Yes, three." "O.k., get them into the bush." '

The way he was telling the story was dead dry.

'That lieutenant colonel,' he ended, 'is now a corporal in the catering corps.'

He proceeded to go into all the politics of UNITA, all the political reasoning of his organization; and I must admit that he did talk a lot of sense about the reasons for the struggle and so on. He was saying that he had a council, and that his council had to agree with any policy decision before it could be implemented. 'My chief accountant here,' he said, turning to one of the lieutenant colonels beside him, 'does all the tallying of the books, and the figures come out right.' The chief accountant answered him in English and they talked man-to-man, but there was no doubt as to who was the boss.

'I have had to put a lot of pressure on the council to get them to agree to release you,' he said, taking this as an example of the way the decision-making was done in UNITA. 'This is about the last time I will be able to do it. The men in the field are fighting for independence from the Marxist government and they are getting a bit cheesed off because they are taking a lot of risks to capture prisoners and all we do, once they have captured them, is to bring them down to Jamba, fill them full of good food and good cheer, and then release them. The council have now decided that the next hostages captured will have to be held indefinitely, to avoid damaging the morale of our troops in the field.'

He turned to us: 'Do you realize,' he asked, 'that you were working for a Marxist government?'

'Yes,' we replied.

'Why do you work for them?'

'We work overseas and in a sense we are mercenaries of work,' we explained. 'We go for the highest bidder, and in this case our employers were offering a dollar contract. Plus there are fringe benefits on top of that because of the danger of being captured by UNITA.'

That tickled him pink.

'How much extra do they pay you, then, if you are captured by UNITA?' he asked, chuckling.

'It isn't a matter of whether you are captured or not,' I explained. 'We get an extra bonus generally because of the severe conditions we have to live in, restrictions on travel and so forth. When you add all these things together, it comes out as a good salary, sometimes twice as much as a normal overseas contract. We have to take a chance, agreed, and sometimes it pays and sometimes it doesn't. Speaking personally, I have taken a lot of chances, and this is the first one that hasn't paid off.'

'Will we see you personally back in Angola?' asked Savimbi.

'No,' I said, 'I wouldn't come back to Angola, because if I got captured again I'd be in trouble.'

'*You . . . are . . . dead . . . right*,' he said slowly, stressing each word, just like that.

But he didn't intimidate me, even if that was his intention.

'I have taken my chance and I have lost,' I said, 'so that is the end of it.'

'If I asked you to come back to Angola when it is a democratic government, would you come back?'

'I will say as I said before,' I replied. 'If the money is right, I will be back. But if the money is no good, I won't be back.'

'So you don't owe any allegiance to the people of Angola?'

'No,' I said. 'They want my expertise, so they pay for it. Whether I stay or go makes no odds to them, because once I go they will bring someone else in. Allegiance to Angola doesn't come into it.'

'Don't you have any feelings about Angola at all?' he asked, sounding almost hurt.

'I wouldn't say that,' I replied truthfully. 'You can't live in a place and not go away without some feelings. I think it is a beautiful country, particularly some of the country we walked through – absolutely fantastic. Later on when Angola is free I would like to go back into the interior on foot and see it again.'

That appeared to amuse him too.

'I have heard of mad dogs and Englishmen,' he said, 'but speaking for myself I don't think I'd like to go back that way again. Mind you, I have walked that trail personally three times.'

Savimbi is no fool, and I think he preferred frank answers to bullshit. When we had first been introduced, the Captain had been all over him, telling him, when asked how things were, that everything had been 'wonderful, excellent, perfect, absolutely no complaints at all'; and always butting in with expressions of approval as the President explained UNITA's policy. So in the end Jonas just totally ignored him, and he did not even bother to ask the Captain whether he would come back to Angola or not. But he asked Al, and he asked John.

'No,' said John, 'but then I already live in South Africa.'

'No,' said Al, 'I am not even coming back to the continent of Africa ever again.'

John gave the impression of being a bit shocked and stunned; he never volunteered anything, just answered questions. But Al did not appear overawed by the man at all. 'He seemed a nice guy,' was all he said afterwards.

At the end of about three-quarters of an hour of conversation I put my hand up. Savimbi had been talking about communications.

'Yes?'

'With regard to communications,' I said, 'we have not got a

clue as to what is going on, because we have no radio; and we've had no radio contact at all with the outside world for two-and-a-half months. Is it possible to get a radio?'

'I don't know,' replied the President. 'Let me speak with my security men.'

'O.k., can I ask another favour?' I said, plucking up my courage.

'Yes.'

'Is it possible for us to have a toothbrush?'

'A toothbrush? But you have been here for four weeks!'

'I know,' I said, 'but we haven't got a toothbrush. We did manage to borrow the padre's razor, which we all share. So that is not a problem. A toothbrush is.'

'I am going to look into this,' said Savimbi with a face of thunder. 'You will have a toothbrush within twenty minutes of leaving here.'

After the President had left, everyone crowded round and said to me, 'You were right to ask him for this and that.' And, sure enough, within twenty minutes we were issued with brand-new toothbrushes in cellophane packing. So somebody got a roasting; and whenever we wanted anything from the major after that, it was, 'Look, get us this – or else we are going to tell Joe,' which went down in a good-humoured way.

That night, after we had come back from the meeting, we were so keyed up that we did not sleep a wink. This was not because we had met the great man, though Paul told us afterwards that he had felt in awe of Savimbi, and certainly the feeling of command came across pretty strongly in his presence. Personally I admired Joe because he had a hard trail to follow. Looking at other African countries with guerrilla movements, they are nearly always vicious ones, unlike UNITA; and UNITA's good behaviour I put down to Joe personally. I would call him a real gentleman. But the reason we were so keyed up was because of something he had told us, which came as a shock – a real shock.

'We don't know,' I had said when asking for the radio, 'if you have had bad publicity and press or the opposite, or no comment at all.'

'I will tell you this,' Savimbi had replied. 'You are big news outside Angola. Your names are mentioned on the Voice of America and the BBC World Service. Your actual names mentioned.'

'No,' we had said, disbelievingly.

'Am I a man to joke?' he had retorted.

'No.'

'Well, you believe me!'

When we were captured, we had had the impression that we would not receive any publicity – not that we were looking for any – because as far as British hostages captured in Angola went, there had on the previous occasion been seventeen and this time round there had only been three of us. And in any case, who is interested second time round?

When we got a radio the next day, we nearly wore the dial out trying to pick up the news. There was no mention of us at all, so for a week all went flat. Then, one evening, we just managed to pick up a BBC report, not mentioning our names personally but saying that three Britons held by UNITA were going to be released imminently. That was another night when, understandably, we never slept a wink. For at long last after the hardships and tribulation, and after the even greater hardships – in their way – of boredom and total ignorance of what was going on, our ordeal was clearly drawing to its close.

Chapter IX

Release

But, as had so often happened before when our hopes had been raised, nothing happened. There was a further burst of excitement a couple of nights later when, at 2 a.m., the major came stalking in and switched on the light.

'Come on, lads, out of bed,' he announced. 'The tailor wants to measure you.'

'Two o'clock in the morning? The tailor?' we asked, unbelievingly.

'Yes, it is very urgent you get this done.'

We all sleepily got to our feet and were measured, and we were told that within 24 hours our new clothes would be ready.

Blow me, at 2 a.m. on the dot the following night they burst in again with brown shirts and brown striped trousers, and up out of bed we had to shoot, again, to try them on.

'What is this all for?' we asked.

'You are going to be released shortly. You must look tidy,' we were told.

So next morning we were anticipating great things. But, as usual, nothing happened. However, release was definitely in the air, our morale was up, and we were all being treated very well – except for the Portuguese. At the meeting Savimbi had been scathing about the Portuguese. First of all, he had talked the whole time in English, so we and the Americans and the Filipinos could follow him, but the five Portuguese just sat there not understanding a thing. Secondly, when complaining about the bad publicity UNITA had received in the British press and mentioning the good publicity in the American press, he had just dismissed the Portuguese: 'Portugal . . . like that,' he had said, with a contemptuous wave of his hand.

By this time we, the Americans and the Filipinos were allowed to mingle freely, but the Portuguese were still confined to their hut. Worse, there had been no mention on the Portuguese services of any release date for them, and Savimbi had more or less indicated to the Portuguese that he had no clue at all as to when they would be released.

The most recent captive, the Diamang courier, was a bag of

nerves, shaking all over the place. If you called him 'a Portuguese arsehole', he would burst into tears. The Portuguese do show their emotions – but not usually to that extent. It was probably from having been the only white man among a load of blacks for months. But the electrician was in an even worse state. He had an abscess up his nose, and the whole of his face was swollen; the swelling had closed his eye. He used to sit there weeping. He was really depressed, and we thought he might be going to commit suicide. So we went to the major.

'We believe this guy is mentally disturbed,' we told him, '– that he is going to do himself in.'

'That will be just one less Portuguese to bother about,' shrugged the major. That was the way Angolans in general felt about the Portuguese. There were sparks in the air, and in those last two weeks the Portuguese did get badly neglected.

The other two Portuguese were more worried about what they were going to do once released, because they were Diamang's employees. Diamang only functions in Angola, and they knew they would have to sign a pledge to UNITA upon release that they would never return to work in the country – a pledge that would be their death warrant if they ever broke it and were captured again. The economy in Portugal was such a disaster that they would have been hard pushed to find any employment there; so at this stage they were turning much more courteous and friendly and asking us to look out for jobs for them, anywhere.

Bushbunny, however, had quite a different set of preoccupations. He was not perturbed at all by the fact that UNITA had not told the Portuguese anything about their release date. He just lay on his bed with a crooked smile on his face. He was quite happy to remain in Angola for the rest of his life.

'Who is going to pay for my flight?' he would say. 'I'm not employed by any company, so don't let them bother, let them just leave me here. If they do send me back to Portugal, what am I going to do? I have no house, nowhere to live, no job. All I can do is go round begging. I don't want to go back, not to that.'

One Monday night about 6.30 p.m. the major came in again.

'Get your new shirts on, your new trousers and your plimsolls,' he said.

'Where are we going?'

'Just a little trip.'

We had never been out at night in the dark before since arriving in Jamba, so it seemed a little unusual. A truck collected all of us, careered for about half an hour through the bush, and then drove down a ramp into an underground bunker. There were tables laid out there with sweets, plates piled with sandwiches cut in triangles and, beside them, cans of Coca-Cola.

'Is this for us?' we asked the major.

'No,' he said. 'Just sit still. Don't eat anything.'

We sat there for about half an hour, speculating. We thought it might be another meeting with Savimbi, or perhaps a propaganda lecture – a form of entertainment we had been spared since arriving in Jamba. We nicked the occasional sandwich or sweet as time went by and nothing happened.

Eventually they took us out of there. As they were taking us across to an entrance that seemed to lead to another underground bunker, we passed a truck with a generator on it and I suddenly heard a bloke shout: 'Is that enough power on there, Bernard?'

'Hang on,' I said, registering the language. 'That is a bloody Englishman!'

We looked, and there was a white bloke standing there.

'Who are you?' I asked, amazed.

'BBC.'

We were stunned, gawping like idiots.

'What do you mean, BBC?'

'British Broadcasting Corporation.'

'What are you doing here?' We could still hardly take it in.

'We have come to film three English pillocks,' he replied.

'That's us,' we said, finally registering it all.

'I gathered that,' he grinned.

The major summoned us in, ushering us down the ramp and through the doors at the bottom. The scene that faced us was unreal. There seemed to be hundreds of white people there, with cameras and tripods set up on all sides.

'Jesus,' I said to John and Paul, 'we have got to get organized here.'

Then Peter Sharp from ITN came up. He shook hands.

'This is where the press conference will be,' he explained.

I suppose we had realized by then what it was all about, but only half-consciously.

'Hang on,' I said, 'we just want a couple of minutes on our own, the three of us.'

So we backed off.

'You just say what you think,' the major told us.

'All the same, we'd better be careful what we say politically and about our companies,' I told the lads hastily, before we were ushered forward again and sat down at a long table facing the cameras.

The press conference lasted for about an hour, and it was shattering, it really was. Besides the BBC and ITN, there were Dutch, French, German and Italian television, any number of radio stations, and Reuter's too; but, surprisingly, nothing for the Americans. So they concentrated on us. John just sat there like a zombie with his eyes wide open. He didn't blink, he didn't do anything, he just stared. It was not until the last five minutes that Paul chirped in and started saying his piece. It was left to me to do the talking, and I just blathered on about our capture, how we spent New Year's Eve, and lots of rubbish like that. It was tiring, because all the time I had to bear in mind that we did not want to offend FAPLA or the government, seeing that our companies would still have to go on working in Angola. But even in their questions the press let us off very easily, and so we did not put our feet in it.

When it was all over, a UNITA general there and two lieutenant colonels all came up and shook our hands.

'What are you shaking my hand for?' I asked them.

'You did a good job,' replied our major.

'A good job how?'

'Good publicity for UNITA.'

'Sod UNITA,' I said, in disgust. I had not been doing it for them.

But even so the lieutenant colonels came back with us – partly to share the goodies that the TV crews had dished out, I suspect. We left that conference with three bottles of whisky, three cartons of cigarettes – Rothmans, Marlboro and Benson & Hedges – and with packets of Rowntree fruit pastilles, which were great. We shared all this out with the Filipinos, Portuguese and Americans; and, to give the lieutenant colonels their due, when we ran out of booze they went off and brought some more in. So we had a right ding-dong back at our hut, and I don't think any of us went to bed till way past dawn. We were too keyed up to sleep in any case.

The next day UNITA held its nineteenth anniversary celebrations. They were the reason why Savimbi had delayed our release, to get the international press and the camera crews down to Jamba for us, and then squeeze all the favourable publicity he could out of this event. I have to say it was an impressive occasion. On top of the usual speeches, dancing and chanting there was some of the best military marching I have ever seen, black or white – and I include events like the Trooping of the Colour in London and the Edinburgh Tattoo in Scotland. It was carried out by a group of 200 UNITA troops and lasted for about 20 minutes; they never repeated a manoeuvre, and not a word of command was heard. I watched them like a hawk, and not a single one of those there on parade made a mistake: it was precision. Admittedly they were a bullshit battalion – they wore white gloves and were very smartly turned out, and they had probably trained for this and this alone – but I must say that it really impressed me.

The press was there again, all around us, and they kept coming up and sticking a lens two inches in front of our noses. Eventually a UNITA camera crew joined in too, under the auspices of a lieutenant colonel.

'Can I ask you some questions in English?' he said.

The first question he asked was: 'What do you think of UNITA?'

'Before I was captured I thought you were a bunch of hooligans,' I said, 'and now I think you are a bigger bunch of hooligans.'

'What is this word "hooligan"?'

I tried to explain it. He did not seem impressed.

'What about your treatment?' he asked.

'On the trail you did the best you could,' I replied, 'though you pushed us very hard. You fed us the same food as your troops – almost.'

'What is your attitude to UNITA?'

'I am highly tee'd off with UNITA,' I told him, 'because I have lost a good job with the company I was with, plus a good salary, plus all my personal belongings. I don't thank UNITA for doing that to me. I have been marched 600 miles on foot and transported 600 miles by truck, and I didn't enjoy that at all. I didn't like the food, and I lost a lot of weight. I had diarrhoea and sickness and various other ailments.'

'O.k., o.k.,' he interrupted me, 'finish.'

He wound the film back, and off he went. So he wasn't interested. But somebody had to protest. They were probably thinking that we felt like it was a holiday camp – and it was no holiday camp. I had to get that point across.

The Red Cross eventually did arrive, on the Thursday afternoon. They landed on an airstrip twelve hours' drive away, inside Angola, somewhere near the Botswana border, and drove out to Jamba by truck. There were two Red Cross officials: one doctor, a German, and one administrator, a Swiss, very efficient. They were closeted with UNITA all that afternoon, doing all the official documentation; but the grapevine was working well, and we heard almost immediately that they had arrived and that we were all due to be released the following night . . . all of us, that is to say, except the Portuguese.

The Portuguese were given a really rough ride. On the Friday they were not allowed out, and they were not even allowed to speak to the Red Cross. They kept coming over to our hut: 'Have you heard anything about us being released?' they would ask again and again. We felt sorry for them, but there was nothing we could do, and it was getting bloody monotonous.

'Why don't you just walk over to the Red Cross and ask if you are going to be released, and sod UNITA?' John suggested. But they would not. As luck would have it, the abscess broke in the electrician's nose, and he was in agony. But though we could now have penicillin or any medicine we wanted from the German doctor, who gave us each a pre-release check-up, the electrician could only get minor treatment from the UNITA medic: nothing specific.

We were then taken to an underground bunker to fill in forms and have our documents sorted out before leaving; we were particularly anxious about our passports and the money that had been confiscated from us at Cafunfo. As we were sitting there, a lieutenant colonel came in and I asked him about these. 'They are coming,' he replied. Sure enough, shortly afterwards we were given our documents and the Americans were each given the exact amount of money that had been taken off them – John, Paul and I had had none on us. But when it came to the Filipinos, every document was there, nothing was missing, yet all the money had gone.

'Where is the money for the Filipinos?' I asked the clerk.

'I don't know,' he replied. 'It is lost.'

'You are a bloody *bandido*,' I accused him angrily. 'UNITA are *bandidos*.'

That made him mad. He went out and reported what I had said to the lieutenant colonel.

'Calm down,' everyone else was saying, even the Filipinos, 'or they might not release us.'

'That is beside the bloody point,' I said. 'The Americans get all their money back but not the Filipinos because the Filipinos don't hold any political value. It makes you hopping mad.'

But even though the Filipinos had no joy, the Portuguese did on their problem. Twenty minutes before we were due to leave they were told that they were going to be released too. The Diamang employee went almost mad with joy, dancing up and down all over the place. Bushbunny, poor lad, sat there with a long face. The Red Cross signed for us formally, and at about 8 p.m. we were loaded into two trucks, one for the two Red Cross, the British, the Americans and Portuguese, and the other for the Filipinos. They had put mattresses in the trucks and, compared with the previous lorry trips we had had, it was really comfortable – we had plenty of room and we could stretch our legs out freely.

We drove all through the night. For the first two hours we were certainly travelling south-east towards Botswana; but at about 10 p.m. the Western Star went down, and as it was a moonless night it was hard to say which direction we continued to go in. Just before the star disappeared, our truck, the leading truck, ground to a sudden halt. I was standing up against the headboard, in my favourite position, looking over the cabin, and there, standing in front of the truck caught by the headlights, were a beautiful lion and a lioness. They would not move. It was absolutely great.

Hours later, about 2 a.m., a large bull elephant loomed up out of the darkness; he was coming towards the truck and was in a bit of a panic, probably confused by something approaching him so quickly out of the dark, and he started snorting, grunting, waving his trunk about and flapping his ears. He veered off into the bush, and we could hear him for minutes afterwards, crashing through the undergrowth. So it was not till right at the end of the trip, on the very last leg of our journey, that we had the excitement of seeing big game.

Dawn was breaking as we arrived at an underground village. The only things visible above ground were its grass roofs. At about 7 a.m. we were herded into an underground bunker where long tables, covered with white tablecloths and properly laid out with knives, forks, spoons, glasses, mugs, cups, the lot, were waiting for us. This was UNITA's last, and very special, parting treat. They brought us eggs, bacon, beans, chips, toast, marmalade and cornflakes. We had not had an egg in three months, but we soon made up for that, each of the lads having two or three eggs. We could have as much as we wanted. It was unreal.

An hour later we were sitting around, having finished guzzling, just drinking tea and coffee, when we heard the drone of an approaching aircraft. Everybody downed cups and rushed outside. There was a silver speck coming across the sky. It flew straight over us at about 30,000 feet. That cannot be ours, we thought; it is much too high. Then it turned round and started circling and dropping down. We all rushed out towards the runway, a grass track laid out on chalky ground.

The plane was a Hercules, run by a Swiss company called Transair which had been much involved in rescue operations in Biafra. She came in to land . . . beautiful; stopped opposite us; then she started to turn round on the runway – and, as she did so, one set of wheels buried themselves in the ground and the whole plane listed over.

'Oh Jesus,' we thought as we ran out and gazed in dismay at the great big hole the wheels were in, 'we are going to spend another week here digging this thing out.' It seemed too cruel to be frustrated like this at the last moment, but it was typical, in a way, of the whole of our journey down through Angola – the sort of disappointment we had almost come to expect.

This time, however, it was not to turn out like that. The crew shooed us out of the way, started up the engines again and gave them full blast forward. Thereupon the Hercules came lurching out of the hole into the bush, sending bits of grass and twigs flying in all directions. Then she reversed out of the bush on to the runway again and closed all engines down. While the crew were inspecting for damage – thank God there wasn't any – all the UNITA lieutenant colonels came up to shake our hands and say goodbye, including the one who had been in charge of the document distribution the day before.

'You must believe we are not bandits,' he said to me.

'O.k., Colonel,' I replied, 'but you tell me where the money is.'

'I don't know. It is lost.'

'Look,' I said, 'I don't want an argument but I don't believe you. You manage to find it for the Americans but when it comes to the Filipinos it is "lost". We are talking about $13,000 approximately, and that is a lot of money.'

'You didn't have any money,' he said, 'so why are you shouting about it?'

'I know I didn't have any money. That's not the point. It's the Filipinos' money I'm interested in, and it means a lot to them.'

'Why should you be interested in the Filipinos' money?' he asked, nastily.

'They are my people, my responsibility.'

'They are not. They are UNITA's.'

'So it is all right for UNITA to rip them off, take their money, and nobody is allowed to say anything, I suppose?'

'We do not want this mentioned to the press,' he said, beginning to be worried.

'No,' I said firmly, 'you told me and President Savimbi told me that I am to hide nothing from the press at all but just to tell it as it happened. You agree that that is true?'

'Yes, I agree that is true. But do not call us *bandidos*; that is a mistake.'

'O.k., then,' I said, 'you tell me what you are. If you are not bandits over this, what are you then? You tell me.'

It did no good. He got mad, and off he went, refusing to shake hands. My guess is that the Filipinos' money was taken by our first escort battalion, and so there was no chance of their ever getting it back. Unfortunately, though justifiably, this dust-up was my last encounter with UNITA, and my final, sour memory of Angola.

John and I were the last two to board the Hercules. After it had taken off and the seatbelts were unfastened, the Swiss stewardess brought us soft drinks and sandwiches; then we started throwing off our clone-like UNITA clothes and putting our own stuff back on again. We were dancing up and down the aisle – with barely a glance down as we left Angola, and UNITA and FAPLA, and all their quarrels, and a good part of our own lives, far, far behind us.

Postscript

Two hours later we arrived at Johannesburg Airport to be faced by a second, and much tougher, press conference in the VIP lounge. Then we all went our separate ways – John's South African wife was there to meet him, and Trans-American Airways had flown out Al's family, and Paul's family from England, and the Captain's wife (to my astonishment she was a cracker, a lovely-looking woman, about 45). But I never said goodbye to him; by this time we weren't on those terms.

Intraco had arranged for a representative to meet myself and the Filipinos, and this guy whisked us off to the Holiday Inn just outside the airport. As soon as we were out of the airport he told me that Jasper – my translator/secretary and security man, who had left Cafunfo just before UNITA attacked – had been found in a back alley in Luanda with his throat cut. What a waste . . . I often wonder if he would have survived with us, had he stayed.

Everybody had a separate room at the hotel, with fruit, flowers, whisky, gin, beer and soft drinks all laid on, courtesy of Intraco, especially for us.

'The first thing we do,' I told the lads, 'everybody soak in the bath, and I will meet you down here at about 4 o'clock.' But in fact the first thing I did was to phone Lynn and the girls in England. After that, I was into that bath for two hours, enjoying the hot water and the soap suds. I came out all crinkly. Then a cold shower after – that was fantastic – and a lie-down between clean white sheets. But we were not allowed into Johannesburg, as we had planned, because the Filipinos had no identification – at least, that was the reason given. In the hotel restaurant that night, as soon as they realized who we were, it was dinner on the house; and Intraco had dished out over 2000 rand for drinks. 'You can spend what you like in the hotel,' the representative had said, 'but don't go berserk.'

'Sod it,' I thought, 'this is going to be a night-and-a-half, this one.' I think only three of us managed to walk back to our rooms, eventually; the rest had to be carried.

On Sunday we dozed and relaxed and recovered. On

Monday, after taking all the Filipinos' measurements – they were still not allowed into the city – the company bought them all new jackets, trousers, coats, shoes, everything. Then I went to see the British Consul, to get myself a temporary passport, and bought myself a whole new outfit, too.

Intraco gave all of us our normal salaries from the day of our capture till the day of our release – which for some of the Filipinos meant a virtual bonus of as much as £3-£3,500. They also gave me £1000 compensation for everything I had lost and a first-class ticket back to the UK. I flew back that Tuesday on a British Airways flight and was ushered first off the plane at London, Heathrow to be met by a Foreign Office man and my wife and daughters (Susan and Lisa). Then I was faced with a sort of shouting press interview before being whisked off by taxi to the TV AM studios, where my brother met me – he had come down from Leicestershire with the family to pick me up. I was quite experienced with interviews by then; Dennis Healey was on the programme, and I found myself disagreeing with him, in public and without embarrassment, about Angola. Even when I got back to Burton-on-the-Wolds, press and radio people were on the line constantly for the next two days.

The Foreign Office had been very helpful to both Lynn and myself; they had done a great job. The man from the FO who had met me, Mr Livesey, rang up to ask if everything was o.k.; and he rang up a week later to ask me for a debrief next time I came down to London.

So I went down to London, and there I met Paul again; it was quite odd to see him in decent clothes. Our debriefing session went on for about two hours; it was attended by about three or four junior Ministers and quite a lot of high officials from the Foreign Office. I had to go through all the weaponry that UNITA was using, and their military tactics, because I had been in the army myself. They were interested in all of that.

The next excitement was when Intraco rang me up to say that the Ambassador of the Philippines wished to meet me. I phoned him. 'Would you please come down to lunch?' he said. So I went to his residence, just behind St James's Palace; there were maids and other servants all over the place, and I felt a bit of a Charlie because, what with about ten silver knives this side and ten silver forks that side, it was right out of my line. We had traditional Filipino food – boiled salmon and rice – and I was thanked for looking after the Filipinos and told that if ever

I wanted to visit the Philippines, the Ambassador himself would arrange a trip for me.

'Right, I'll take you up on that in about a year's time,' I said.

I sent Al photographs of the family and we agreed to send each other New Year's cards in remembrance of the last new year. But the Captain, I have heard, went into a mental institution when he returned to the United States; and now he is suing Trans-American for loss of earnings and loss of job, and I hear they are suing him for landing when he should not have done, so I should think there are big court cases going on.

Trans-American pulled out of the Lunda Province operation immediately after their loss; but Mr Hilinger was very active, and almost immediately he brought in two Hercules as Intraco planes, with Filipino crews who had served in Vietnam. If UNITA ever take over the country, Intraco could be in trouble; but Mr Hilinger is a very well-organized guy. The expats in Angola jokingly say he may even have his own contacts with UNITA – he is that sort of man. Intraco now has a new operation in the Congo, supplying vehicles and timber-felling equipment there; but the Angola operation is still one of Hilinger's most important contracts to date.

Since release quite a few of the Filipinos have written to me, often asking me whether I could try to find them jobs . . . but there just aren't any such jobs. I know it is a struggle for them to make a living.

As for myself, after a bit of a rest at home, I got another job – this time in Zambia, rather a dull posting by contrast to Angola, but a very pleasant and interesting country.

John, as far as I know, is still in South Africa, and Paul is at home in England. On the march we agreed that if we could ever put our diary to use, write articles or a book or anything, we would share out whatever proceeds came in between the three of us. And now we have this book.

I hope that if I have said anything in these pages that they violently disagree with, John and Paul will not hold it against me; for though it is the story of all three of us, indeed of all twenty-three of us, I have had to tell it in my own way, and according to my feelings, as best as I could. But I am sure of one thing: it is an experience that none of us, and we were all ordinary blokes who took part in it, will ever forget or want to forget.